Ideas for
the Working Classroom

Ideas for the Working Classroom

Classroom Practices in Teaching English
Vol. 27

Kent Gill, Editor,
and the Committee on Classroom Practices

National Council of Teachers of English
1111 W. Kenyon Road, Urbana, Illinois 61801-1096

Grateful acknowledgment is made for permission to reprint:
"First Snow in Alsace" from *The Beautiful Changes and Other Poems*, copyright 1947 and renewed 1975 by Richard Wilbur, reprinted by permission of Harcourt Brace & Company.

Cover Design: R. Maul

Interior Design: Doug Burnett

Production Editor: Michelle Sanden Johlas

Manuscript Editors: Humanities & Sciences Associates

NCTE Stock Number: 22574–3050

Contents

Introduction

For this, the twenty-seventh volume in the Classroom Practices series, we wish to celebrate successful teaching practices in English and the language arts—to reaffirm the competence that resides at the classroom level. We present these essays as representative of the efforts of ingenious, dedicated teachers everywhere, who use sound pedagogy and creativity to prepare student-centered activities. There is indeed something to celebrate!

Late in 1990, the committee completed its review of seventy-eight papers, offered as descriptions of successful classroom practice. Shortly thereafter, I read the article, "The Best Schools in the World," in the December 2, 1991, issue of *Newsweek* (47–48). It seemed like serendipity that the qualities which marked these acclaimed international programs were the same qualities that had drawn us to the best reports of English classroom practices:

> A natural system of learning by doing rather than by reductive drill.
>
> A nurturing of learner independence and responsibility.
>
> An integration of academic disciplines or branches of disciplines that focuses on theme, meaning, or idea.
>
> A collaboration of learners.
>
> An emphasis on practicality and connection with real life.
>
> An exploitation of error for learning rather than for penalty.

This conjunction of circumstances was most reassuring. It attested to something we already believed—that good English teachers do indeed know what they are doing.

The evidence in these papers reveals teachers who learn from their experiences—inventing, adapting, and refining practices as they are guided by their students' responses. Even though they are not being rigidly experimental, they are applying the essence of research in developing and fine-tuning their teaching behavior and the activities they propose for their classes.

In these descriptions of classroom practice, the writers provide us, of course, with the sequences, the procedures, and the materials, so that we can replicate their lessons. Then they persuade us with samples of student work and direct reports of student response. They also help us to understand why they developed these particular practices in the first place; they do so by underscoring theoretical bases about how children best learn and how language is best taught.

These descriptions of high-quality practices share certain hallmarks. They speak with authority, each saying, "This worked for me." They carry no guarantee, but they do offer much promise—and they honor and respect the students who were the subjects of instruction. These reports reveal true *educators,* classroom teachers who are drawing performance out of their students, rather than pouring education into them. Furthermore, these accounts demonstrate that literacy and literary mastery are but different bands on the same spectrum.

Our authors offer their practices to the profession with humility. If an idea intrigues you or applies to your teaching situation, you are encouraged to try it. Shape it to your situation; make it fit your own teaching style and your own students. Expect to modify and build on it. If the practice works well for you, you are welcome. Your only obligation is to share *your* next good idea with your colleagues.

Kent Gill
Camp Sherman, Oregon

I Respecting Ourselves and Others

As language arts teachers, we know that our students have lives beyond the classroom, lives in which they are developing much of their character and personality. They draw on family and group values, on the cultural practices that surround them, even on prejudices. It is wise for us to recognize and build on these circumstances, making them useful elements in successful learning experiences.

One of our major societal concerns is how people relate to one another, how differences among folks are perceived and acted upon. The language arts classroom can contribute significantly in helping young people respond respectfully and positively to those they see as being somehow different. A fringe benefit of this is a more harmonious, productive classroom and society in general.

A very real, present-day crisis for youth involves the facts of massive social disorganization—dysfunctional families, gangs, alcohol and drugs, promiscuity, abuse. If they are lucky, those most affected may somehow find a sense of worthiness and self-respect. Their chances for that discovery can be enhanced through the experiences and relationships in their school classrooms. Therefore, we see, in the present collection of essays, classroom teachers deliberately designing English "lessons" that will help young people build self-esteem as well as respect for others.

To this end, Beverly A. McColley, in "Diversity and Community in the Classroom," capitalizes on the paradox of discovering community in the very differences students bring to her classroom. She finds that her students function best in a climate where a sense of collective class identity permits the individual members to be different. Her characterization of the teacher as orchestra leader is an apt metaphor.

In "Sharing Lives," Edythe H. Schwartz uses memoirs as a powerful tool for helping students to ask questions and challenge assumptions and to begin to know human issues from the inside. Her examples, drawn from various points in the school term, demonstrate the progressive sophistication of this social- and self-awareness program.

Rose Cherie Reissman, in "Cresting for Character and Community," has the students in her inner-city classroom develop family crests, not only as a lesson in symbolization, but even more so as a means to enhancing one's self-image.

In a spritely presentation entitled "A Positively Rewarding Experience," Beverly Wilkins shows us a simple, positive reinforcement becoming an important classroom tool.

Theodore F. Fabiano and F. Todd Goodson, teaching in a sheltered, suburban Kansas high school, share "The Fifty-Mile Radius Project" that led their students to explore a diverse set of neighboring communities for a collection of meaningful, personal encounters. As a result, the students broadened their own cultural horizons while applying the lessons of their English class to the real world in significant ways.

1 Diversity and Community in the Classroom

Beverly A. McColley
Norfolk Academy, Norfolk, Virginia

For years, we have been hearing about cultural diversity and individual learning styles. To be sure, education must adapt itself to the characteristics of diversity; yet it seems to me that there is an underlying need for *community* before diversity can flourish. If each student is to make a unique contribution, there must be some collective, embracing identity that makes it safe and desirable to be different. This, then, has been my approach to diversity: establish a collective identity that supports and encourages the individual.

There are many ways to establish community. Eliot Wigginton has students recall and assess good teaching methods they have experienced, and in their sharing, create a new community with a positive orientation. John Dixon encourages students to share stories, particularly their reading histories, building a collective identity through shared personal narrative. Both Dixon and Wigginton use small-group interaction almost immediately as they establish these learning communities. I have tried these techniques myself and found them to be successful. Like Wigginton, I put students into small groups, asking them to recall and share positive learning experiences, and to generate a list of traits that typify a good teacher. After the small-group experience, the students go on to compile a list of traits to be displayed in the room throughout the term—a visible reminder that each of us is a participant in creating and developing a learning community. John Dixon's idea about reading histories works in a similar way. Once again, my students share in small groups, this time talking about favorite childhood books and early reading memories. The first level of sharing takes place in an intimate setting, the small group; the next level of sharing takes place within the class as a whole. As students tell their stories, individuals are affirmed and the community develops, its fabric enriched by each narrative, each a part now of the community's collective memory and identity.

Another thing I like to do at the outset is to identify talents within the group that can be used to serve our collective needs. I like to have the students choose artists, photographers, actors, teachers, and editors from amongst themselves. Throughout the year, I keep a scrapbook for each class, including samples of their art and writing, as well as snapshots of them writing, working in groups, or performing. Each addition to the scrapbook helps to build a sense of community. In addition to the scrapbook, I create a class library of videotapes, capturing students as they give oral reports, perform plays, or present "Reader's Theater." Not only the individual performances, but also the collaborative work they do to provide background music, graphics, and credits for the videotape help them build their sense of community.

Whenever possible, I allow those with teaching ability to teach segments of the class; those who like to perform are encouraged to serve as emcees or actors; those who like to draw are asked to make covers or illustrations for writing portfolios, bookmarks for novels, or graphics for videotapes; and those who like to edit are allowed to help others find problems in their writing. If each student feels useful and knows that his particular talents and uniqueness are appreciated, then everyone feels a part of the community in the truest sense. The foundation of this approach is to identify their respective talents and then create an environment where each is happy making her unique contribution to the whole. Of course, report cards do establish academic hierarchies in the class, but it is still possible to forge a group identity that values individuals for who they are and what they contribute. This means that both the underachiever and the overachiever can earn recognition from their peers, as well as the freedom to take risks and make mistakes.

To create this kind of environment requires a variety of teaching strategies, moving from large to small groups and back again, from individual to group performances, from personal to collaborative writing. Students work in pairs or groups to write dialogues, plays, or peer evaluations. Frequently, when a group is unable to complete an assignment during the class period, I have the group choose one responsible member to finish the assignment on their behalf. Students take turns in completing the group's tasks, showing pride in what they produce on behalf of their community.

In this setting, the teacher is not a performer, but a facilitator, who allows students to teach, direct, coach, and perform for one another. In this community, the teacher is no longer the soloist, but rather the conductor of an orchestra, one who guards the community from chaos, highlights individual performances, and enables each unique offering to become part of a meaningful whole. To me, this is the most sophisticated teaching of all, when the students take charge of their learning and discipline, under the teacher's skilled and subtle guidance. As students leave the classroom at the end of the year, they carry with them not only what they have learned about literature, writing, and performing, but also their memories of a forged community that transcended their differences.

In this approach, grades are as important as individual successes, yet the community is valued, too. As we realize how tiny our planet truly is, how cherished our resources, and how interdependent our lives, surely this experience of community in the classroom is a way not only to encourage diversity but also to greet the future. To welcome differences is, simultaneously, to create community. Surely, this paradox lies at the heart of good teaching.

2 Sharing Lives

Edythe H. Schwartz
California State University at Sacramento

On this first day of class, Marta sits in the last seat on the right, her lips slightly apart, her eyes penetrating, as I read aloud: "In English my name means hope. In Spanish it means too many letters. It means sadness; it means waiting. . . . At school they say my name funny as if the syllables were made out of tin and hurt the roof of your mouth. But in Spanish my name is made out of a softer something, like silver. . . ." This brief excerpt from Sandra Cisneros's memoir, *The House on Mango Street* (1984), is one of several pieces I will read today to my human development students. I read to offer a taste before the feast, a feast of lives my students will read and write about in the upcoming weeks. These works—memoirs by writers from diverse cultural backgrounds— form the tapestry in which I weave the material of this course, a course that leads students through the life span, a course that examines theories, research, and principles of development in the context of the real and significant social environments of individual lives.

Marta stretches forward, eager to hear more. Later, as I stack my books, preparing to leave the classroom, Marta stops me. She picks up *The House on Mango Street* and, quickly scanning the pages, asks, "Where did you find this book?" "It was a gift," I tell her, "from a friend who knows Hispanic literature." As she slowly hands me the book, Marta murmurs quietly, "Things like this happened to me. I didn't know there are women, Hispanic women like me, who write books." I think about Marta's telling words. Of all the goals I have for transforming these literary works into course content, the ones I consider most crucial are highlighted by Marta's comments: to provide students from diverse ethnic and socioeconomic backgrounds—students still visible in small numbers on our campus—with a feeling of being nurtured, a validation for who they are, and a sense that the university is their place.

Students arrive in my classroom with a rich diversity of heritage and experience. For these students, reading memoirs such as Annie Dillard's *An American Childhood* (1987), selections from Alice Walker's *In Search of Our Mother's Gardens* (1983), as well as Cisneros's work, presents an opportunity to engage personally with another life, thereby enriching their own. Belenky et al. (1986) argue that fostering such "connected knowing" or "knowing on the inside" is essential for real understanding of complex issues. I hope to provide my students with access to the knowledge of others, through reading, talking, and writing about other people's lives. I hope to enable them to challenge their own assumptions, ask searching questions, and examine the writer's purpose and methods. And perhaps students' pleasure in the text will also stretch and empower them to think creatively and to write with strength.

As I design response activities for specific sections of each text, I keep in mind my goals to have students feel integrated, not isolated, in the university setting; examine development in social and cultural contexts; personally engage with the text; and write to clarify their understanding of concepts. Students write these pieces in class, share them orally in small groups, and collect them in a response log throughout the semester. Although I periodically skim selections from students' logs and, on sticky tags, offer brief written comments (e.g., "I agree; Cisneros's short sentences do punctuate her meaning"), I do not grade this writing (although I do assign it credit as an incentive). By not grading, I effectively create the nonthreatening setting that Fulwiler (1979) considers essential if student writers are to rehearse ideas, take risks, and write fluently.

Early in the semester, I use writing prompts that call for limited analysis; later, I use more complex prompts that address specific issues. By designing increasingly challenging activities, I support students' development through Bloom's (1956) levels, from knowledge and application toward analysis, synthesis, and evaluation. To illustrate, I will describe student responses to several prompts for Cisneros's *House on Mango Street.*

Week Three

We are studying genetic transmission. To look at physical traits that might be inherited, I have students read Cisneros's piece, "Hairs" (1984): "Everybody in our family has different hair. My papa's hair is like a broom . . . and me, my hair is lazy . . . Nenny's hair is slippery— slides out of your hand. And Kiki . . . has hair like fur" (10). I then have the students write to the prompt: "How I Got My Hair." They write for five minutes. They share their ideas, concluding that there cannot be one gene for hair color, that it is a polygenic trait which can also be multifactorial, such as when a person with light brown hair becomes blond in the summer, or when a person's hair color or texture changes as a result of illness or a specific drug treatment. Georgia identifies her red tresses as a deliberately arranged, multifactorial trait. Students are most interested in changes they have experienced themselves. Amy's passage is about inheriting blond, straight hair that changed through time to brown, curly hair. She wants to know what causes such changes. This is a good lead-in to discussing gene switches and timetables. I wrap up the class by reexamining how meiosis contributes to genetic variation.

Week Twelve

The topic is adolescence. I begin the week by introducing the normal sequence of pubertal changes in males and females. This week students will write three pieces on consecutive class days, in response to Cisneros's "Hips" (1984), where Cisneros begins:

> One day you wake up and they are there. Ready and waiting like a new Buick with the keys in the ignition . . . ready to take you where? . . . They're good for holding a baby when you're cooking . . . You need them to dance, says Lucy . . . If you don't get them you may turn into a man. Nenny says this and she believes it . . . She is this way because of her age . . . They look like roses, I continue . . . the bones just one day open. Just like that. One day you might decide to have kids and then where are you going to put them . . . bones got to give. But don't have too many or your behind will spread . . . That's how it is, says Rachel. (47–50)

Each of the three response pieces has a different focus. The first is to be a personal memoir, written to the prompt: "Revisit your own adolescence. Write a page describing one powerful event or personal change you experienced at puberty." Students meet in small groups to share pieces. Later, when Mellissa reads to her group, "In the fifth grade I wore the biggest, loosest shirts I could find and always walked with my arms crossed in front of me, hoping no one would notice my protruding breasts," several women laugh in recognition. As I move among the groups, I hear students acknowledge both common and unique emotional responses to pubertal changes. To further explore the dimensions of adolescent change, students write a second piece. The prompt—"What are Cisneros's concerns (worries)? What were yours (as described above)? Draw some parallels between the physical, cognitive, and psychosocial changes Cisneros experienced and those you experienced. Consider how these changes relate to information we have discussed"—focuses on comparing and contrasting experiences and viewing these in the context of prior knowledge. Students' pieces lead to an animated discussion of research findings on the effects of early versus late maturation in males and females.

The final piece based on "Hips" asks students to move into and beyond the text. The prompt—"Choose two of Cisneros's paragraphs and describe how each contributes to your awareness of her impending womanhood. What other themes does Cisneros touch on in this piece? What can you see of Cisneros's future development?"—requires students to offer predictions about Cisneros's life. Some of these predictions will be supported, others negated, in later chapters of *The House on Mango Street*. Again, students meeting in small groups give each other feedback about their ideas and are led to reexamine their own implicit assumptions. When we come together, I move students back to "Hips" to consider, "What specific details help you to feel the writer's experience? How does the writer show appearance, manner, speech, action? What does the writer do to let you into her life?" Students are drawn to their own pieces, to speculate about writing, to contemplate what makes writing come alive.

The End of the Semester

Students have completed a journal of response pieces to selections from each of the memoirs read and have written personal memoirs as well. In small peer groups, they have eagerly engaged with others, stimulating each other's thinking. Their work has also formed the core material for class discussion. Through reading, talking, and writing, perhaps they have moved closer to what Ann Berthoff (1981) calls, "makers of meaning." When students respond to memoirs, they engage, reflect, and write their way to a fuller understanding of development. When students respond to memoirs, they encounter individual lives in settings as diverse as those which exist within and beyond our pluralistic society. Students enter the rich drama of developmental change through the voices of writers who speak of poverty and wealth, of fear and wonder, of joy and disappointment—writers who share multihued, multilayered lives of strength and grace, writers who travel through the life span with students like Marta, making them feel welcome.

Works Cited

Belenky, Mary Field, Blythe McVicker Clinchy, Nancy Rule Goldberger, and Jill Mattuck Tarule. 1986. *Women's Ways of Knowing.* New York: Basic Books.

Berthoff, Ann E. 1981. *The Making of Meaning: Metaphors, Models, and Maxims for Writing Teachers.* Upper Montclair, NJ: Boynton/Cook.

Bloom, Benjamin S., ed. 1956. *Taxonomy and Educational Objectives: Cognitive Domain.* Vol. 1. New York: David McKay.

Cisneros, Sandra. 1984. *The House on Mango Street.* Houston: Arte House.

Dillard, Annie. 1987. *An American Childhood.* New York: Harper & Row.

Fulwiler, Toby. 1979. "Journal Writing Across the Curriculum." In *How to Handle the Paper Load: Classroom Practices in Teaching English, 1979–1980,* edited by Gene Sanford, Chair, and the NCTE Committee on Classroom Practices, 16–19. Urbana: NCTE.

Walker, Alice. 1983. *In Search of Our Mothers' Gardens: Womanist Prose.* San Diego: Harcourt Brace Jovanovich.

3 Cresting for Character and Community

Rose Cherie Reissman
Community School District 25, Flushing, New York

As I stood before the store's display of plastic figures, I overheard a child say, "I really like his shield. Look at how it shows the spider!" The child and I both ended up buying one of the Spiderman™* figures. Perhaps he wanted one for its "neat flashing spider"; I don't know. But I intended to use the figurine as a concrete motivator for what I term my "cresting" unit. The child's enthusiasm had helped me realize how to achieve a central goal in my language arts curriculum—to develop students' sense of self-esteem and community involvement through the use of visual imagery, personal reflection, critical thinking, writing, and oral communication. My Spiderman™ would serve as the starting point for a three-lesson pilot module of activities that met with both student and faculty acclaim.

I introduced this project by displaying various shield and crest patterns to my students. In addition, my Spiderman™ journeyed up and down the rows of my seventh-grade inner-city classroom. I directed the students to select one of the shields or crests and to decide what kind of personality and values were demonstrated in the sample. After a bit of independent reflection, we shared insights about what the symbols represented. I requested that for each trait they cited, the students refer to the particular visual component that revealed the trait to them. Then I distributed crests of British noble families and African tribes. I had the students "read" these emblems, showing how the visual elements of the emblem revealed some trait or value.

Next, the students took a few moments to jot down their own family's crest "inventory": their ethnic, cultural, and religious identities; their likes and dislikes; and their hopes for the future. Two volunteers placed their inventories on the board, and the rest of the class brainstormed appropriate visual symbols to match the inventory items.

---

* Spiderman™ is the exclusive trademark of the Marvel Publications Group, Inc.

Finally, I distributed blank crest forms that students could use to design their own family shields, drawing on their inventories and their family memories and memorabilia.

During the second module, my students exchanged crests they had finished at home (often after consultation with family members). Each student "read" another's crest. They told the designers what they could tell about the family from the symbols on the crest, giving the designers immediate feedback on the success of their crest designs in communicating their identities. Then they discussed the difficulties in making their crests accurately reveal their inventory ideas. We conducted a problem-solving session on some of their common design problems.

Our culminating activity was "What's My Crest?"—a version of the old "What's My Line?" television show. Various final-draft crests were presented to the student panel, which had to interpret the family traits each crest represented. This game-show format gave us yet another way to test the effectiveness of the students' crest designs. Many of the crests were later displayed as a hall exhibit, and several students with computer-graphics skills used a drawing program to create a slide show and printouts of the crests. Students showed pride in their work as they pointed out their crests to friends. Their sense of self-esteem soared, and the group took pride in what it, as a community, had accomplished. Two parents who had been asked to help at home wrote to tell me how much they had enjoyed this family project and the positive relationships it initiated.

4 A Positively Rewarding Experience

Beverly Wilkins
Midway Middle School, Waco, Texas

"I'm sorry I'm late, but I overslept and missed the bus!" (For the third time this week, he fails to mention.)

"My baby sister scribbled all over my assignment. That's why it's late. I had to recopy it."

"Teacher, teacher! My book's in my locker. Can I go get it?"

Sound familiar? As a high school teacher, it was all too familiar to me. I was so distracted by these little annoyances that I knew I had to do something. But what? I thought of Madeline Hunter's (1967; 1989) suggestion to reward the students' positive behavior in order to increase its frequency, then tapering off the rewards as behavior improved. My next thought was,"But my older students won't go for this reward business. They're too sophisticated, or think they are. However, what I've been doing—fussing at them—certainly isn't working."

So began the 1989–90 school year.

"Stickers. That's what I'll use. Who knows, they may go for it. I'm sure they still remember the thrill of getting a star put by their name on an elementary school chart." Older students, I was sure, would be insulted by a gold star or a happy face. Besides, I wanted something unique that would really catch their attention. I checked the catalogs and the educational supply stores and discovered that commercially printed stickers were available. However, they were too expensive for the large quantities I desired and generally not appropriate for older students who exhibited specific behaviors I wanted to reward.

My husband, a computer teacher, suggested I use our Macintosh computer to create my own stickers. With his help, I did just that. I chose address labels that could be run through my computer printer. Address labels come in a variety of sizes, but I found that the 4" x 1/2" labels were easiest to handle. Using the Macintosh, I selected an appropriate graphic, which I pasted into a word-processing program.

Then, I added a catchy slogan, being careful to keep both the graphic and the slogan within the size limitations of the label. Sometimes I used multicolored printer ribbons for added pizazz. The sticker slogans, narrowly focused on specific behaviors, included the following:

"I'm on time to Mrs. Wilkins's class today."

"It's my journal and I love it."

"Mummy, Mummy! I finally finished my note cards."

"I brought my book today."

As time went on, I thought of more and more ideas for stickers:

"I made an A on my test!"

"I passed my test."

"I survived *Macbeth!*"

I gave, and I praised. Hands extended, those "sophisticated" older students begged for more each day. Of course, they did not get one every day, but that added an element of suspense to the classroom routine.

I noticed several immediate benefits from the use of stickers. First, the students really did bring their books to class more often. They also arrived on time more frequently. But best of all, they could see that I cared about them. They had proof—I had given them something. I also noticed a difference in me. Because I was looking for behavior I could reward, I tended to be more positive in my outlook. The students seemed to accept more willingly my criticism of their work, once they knew I also noticed what they were doing right.

The tapering-off process that Madeline Hunter suggested was slightly painful. They loved those stickers! However, if I saw that the behavior I was trying to reinforce was deteriorating, I simply increased the frequency of the reward.

The students attached their stickers to the covers of their journals. When I graded the journals, I gave them extra points for each one they had accumulated. At the end of the year, they even requested a special sticker to go in their memory books. "Go with pride," it proclaimed. And they did.

One morning, at the end of the school year, one of my students, Tom, breezed in. "Will you sign my annual?" he asked.

"Of course I will!"

"And here, this is for you," he said, placing another book on my desk.

It was a Victorian book of days (similar to a journal). "I'm going to come back and check up on you," he said. "If you've been writing in your journal, I may even bring you a sticker!"

Have I written in my journal every day? You bet I have! Tom may come back to check on me. I hope he does.

Works Cited

Hunter, Madeline C. 1989. *Motivation and Reinforcement in the Classroom.* Aptos, CA: Special Purpose Films.

———. 1967. *Reinforcement Theory for Teachers: A Programmed Book.* Segundo, CA: TIP Publications.

5 The Fifty-Mile Radius Project

Theodore F. Fabiano
Blue Valley North High School, Overland Park, Kansas

F. Todd Goodson
University of Kansas

That autumn, the *Kansas City Star* ran an article about our high school, under the headline, "Designer Kids, Designer School?" The story proceeded to examine the students and the atmosphere of our affluent, suburban high school: "Porsches in the student parking lot. Girls who never wear the same designer outfit twice. Kids and their families buckling under the pressure to keep up appearances." The photos accompanying the article included one showing several designer handbags parked on a cafeteria table.

Our students responded hotly to this article, revealing their lack of understanding about other schools and student bodies. They responded to the article with disbelief ("We aren't that way!") or defensiveness ("Our parents work hard for their money. Why should we be ashamed?"). An "us versus them" mentality had clearly developed, with our students becoming defensive and unwilling to consider seriously the contentions of their critics. This experience made it clear that lines had been drawn between rural, suburban, and inner-city areas; groups had created and perpetuated patterns of behavior that restricted the inclusion of people who were different.

As we teachers discussed the article, we realized that many of our students probably were affluent and that there was very little cultural diversity evident in our student body, just as the article had suggested. However, we also realized that we were surrounded geographically by tremendous diversity. In fact, within a fifty-mile radius, there were agricultural, industrial, penal, military, and academic communities, as well as representatives of almost every cultural and ethnic group in the United States. We wanted to allow our students to experience this cultural diversity, to discover and value the people out there.

The Project Plan

We decided to use the idea of a fifty-mile radius for a direct, informal sociological study that would incorporate literature, composition, language study, and oral communication. Since junior English is traditionally the American literature year, we rationalized that this was the logical place for the unit. Fortunately, our juniors, by and large, had access to cars—transportation would be extremely important to our project.

We collected writings by local authors and writings about the area within the fifty-mile radius. These became the readings for the unit. We wanted our students to be writing throughout the unit, but we decided the culminating activity would be a major written project with an oral presentation of the students' experiences and conclusions about their travels.

Being dutiful writing-project folks, we did the assignment ourselves first and used the resulting paper and presentation as a model for the students. We borrowed a video camera, bought some slide film, loaded families into the biggest automobile we could find, and hit the road. The result was a rambling, occasionally embarrassing, unedited videotape, an essay with a loose narrative structure filled with personal observations, and a couple of rolls of film we never got around to developing. We borrowed a phrase and dubbed the project "gonzo travel writing."

Student Introduction to the Project

A brief overview of the project included guidelines, schedules, and grading standards, which were provided about two months before the scheduled presentations. Partners needed to coordinate the schedules, secure the travel arrangements, and prepare the presentations, so plenty of time was required.

The guidelines for the students appear below:

- Visit a town or city within the fifty-mile radius.
- Look for evidence of social and economic qualities.
- Attempt to make contact with local folks.
- Eat at a local restaurant.
- Develop some visual record of the experience: videotape, slides, or photographs.
- Write a gonzo travel paper of at least six pages.

- Make a fifteen-minute presentation to the class that includes visual material as well as material quoted from your paper.
- Use any concrete items you collected to advance the presentation.

We did ask students to choose specific destinations. We copied a local map and provided a copy to each student.

After the initial organizational stage and before the final presentations, the class explored others' views of their school and evaluated these views through discussion and writing. We began with the article from the *Star.* (You can probably find a similar article in your local paper. Ask other teachers or administrators for material that depicts the "outsider's" view of the school. Or you could even send questionnaires to other schools and their students, promising anonymity and encouraging their candid comments about your school.)

From this input, our classes wrote reaction papers, quoting passages they chose to either support or refute. After a first draft and some sharing, we found that the students lacked specific references to passages and comments, thus weakening their arguments, so we had the opportunity to demonstrate the power of quotes within a real context. We skimmed the papers for interesting and controversial opinions, reading them anonymously to the class. The students were surprised to learn that not everyone thought the way they did.

After examining how their school community was viewed, the students turned to their own perceptions of the surrounding areas. They prewrote about their views of nearby towns and villages, using whatever form they wished—some used narratives, some adopted a first-person persona, some did it didactically. The door was open to local literature. We used excerpts from *Bird, Kansas,* a particularly effective collection of fictitious oral histories of small-town life. We were able to look back to our reading of Richard Wright's *Black Boy* as a reference point for both urban and rural life.

The Project in Progress

Students surveyed local literature, dialect studies, and newspaper articles, seeking information about the areas they had chosen to visit. We capitalized on student interest by encouraging them to share anecdotes of their travels and findings. A poster board, noting the destinations of the student travelers, helped to create interest and generate discussions. To do this, we drew an accurate map of the fifty-mile area and affixed arrows with student names and classes. We found that students from different classes, but with similar destinations, compared notes and shared insights when they discovered each other on the map.

The Presentations

We originally scheduled fifteen-minute presentations for each group, but quickly discovered that visual materials required setup time, so the presentations were running longer than anticipated. Students were eager to seek more information about their classmates' travel adventures, so they asked lots of questions. For our first run, we were flexible with time so that everyone could realize the most benefit.

Student Response

The student papers reflected some of the best writing we had seen all year. We believed that the quality was related to the exceptional development of information that allowed the students to feel confident in telling their stories. Their papers reflected discovery and creation; the most forceful aspect was the gonzo quality of liveliness.

Two students who chose to buy groceries for their required meal wrote:

> We got a barbecue bag, buns, ground beef, plates, napkins, ketchup and mustard, a lighter, and Doritos. Of all these items, the ground beef was the most interesting. It was packaged just like sausage, and on the side in very fine print it read: "Meat will return to original color after exposure to air for ten minutes." Kinda' makes you wonder.

At the conclusion of the project, we had students assess what they had learned and offer us some direction for revising the project for next year. Here are some passages reflecting student reaction to the project:

- My parents were impressed that I was excited . . . It opens up some feelings and thoughts.
- As corny as it sounds, I did learn from getting to see a small town first-hand.
- After the project was turned in, I believe I stayed with a yearning to continue to explore in this area. Because of this assignment, I have become much more involved in Hispanic organizations in Kansas and have made good friends.
- [The project] gives us some variety in the daily school projects, and it is variety which keeps learning interesting.

We noted students opening up, appreciating the shift in school methodology, and gaining more interest in other people. We are convinced that this project is an exciting way to get older high school students out of their narrow surroundings and into the world at large. At the very least, the project can help to enliven the study of English. And at best, it begins to break down some barriers between groups in our society through contact and, we hope, understanding.

Work Cited

"Designer Kids, Designer School?" 1991. *Kansas City Star:* E1, E2, cols. 1–2.

II Exploring Social Issues

Contemporary social issues challenge our understanding and demand our attention at every turn. Yet we English teachers rarely exploit these issues as a relevant context for applying the lessons of the language arts. We note instead that the syllabus does not permit us to study AIDS or abortion or air pollution. We rationalize that such studies are the business of the social sciences, that we do not have the materials, that we barely have time to get to *Macbeth* or introductory adverbial clauses. We may accurately anticipate administrative timidity, parental complaint, or community disapproval, and opt for the safety and security of a conservative curriculum.

Even so, the skillful use of a social issue topic can produce a grand English lesson. Students can become deeply interested and involved in an issue that is already important to them. Social issues can seize students by giving them something real and tangible and significant, qualities they sometimes have trouble finding in Chaucer or Twain. Certainly, a societal problem poses important opportunities to do research and reading in contemporary and historical materials, to communicate orally and in writing, to activate a whole range of thinking skills, and to apply work skills to the completion of a wide-ranging study of an issue. All of these skills are at the core of learning in the English class.

To capitalize on the motivational and academic values in using social issues, Jim Burke has developed a high school term project, actively involving his sophomores. They each select a single issue and undertake an intensive study of it. His students use current materials, interviews and surveys, writing and speaking, all in a workshop setting. In "Investigating Society's Problems in the English Class," they offer lively reports to their classmates and develop a term paper.

At the college level, we offer two examples of tackling difficult and controversial issues. In "Objectivity and Prejudice in Writing about AIDS," Gerald F. Luboff describes a series of research-writing activities about AIDS that allows students to confront their ignorance and prejudices and to move on to a more objective, knowledgeable stance. In "Introducing Gay and Lesbian Issues in Freshman Composition," Thomas Dukes uses a cautious, careful approach to gay and lesbian issues that moves students to examine and possibly modify their stereotypical views through reading, viewing, thinking, talking, and writing.

6 Investigating Society's Problems in the English Class

Jim Burke
Burlingame High School, Burlingame, California

I live in San Francisco, a city rife with social problems, but I teach in Castro Valley, a small, quiet suburban town in the East Bay area. Walking to school along Castro Valley's quiet suburban streets, lined with houses whose value has skyrocketed during the past few years, many students at my school probably find it difficult to imagine the homeless people I drive by each morning on my way to work, or the waste disposal problems, or the individuals ravaged by AIDS in the hospitals and on the streets. Therefore, I feel a commitment to increasing my sophomore students' awareness of our societal problems—problems they may have ignored or do not even know exist.

I accomplished this last year by having my sophomores embark on an involved, multifaceted project that lasted an entire quarter. We worked on this project, entitled, simply, "Social Problems," while continuing to study the literature required for our English course.

Brainstorming Possible Problems

We began the project with in-class brainstorming and individual listing of different social problems. Several topics the students came up with were common to many of the lists: the greenhouse effect, homelessness, pollution. Scanning their lists I could see that several of them also included abortion, gun control, and capital punishment. We got to work by making a master list of these topics on the board. I put up whatever they said, but I did not feel ready to draw the fine distinction between problems and issues. By the time a student named Brett called out "gun control," it seemed that we had exhausted their ideas.

I asked Brett how he arrived at gun control as a social problem. "Well, it seems like so many people are getting killed with guns these days," he said. "So are the guns the problem here, or is there something else?" I asked. Andrea pointed out that guns were not the problem, but that one problem society faces is a serious, increasing crime rate. "So, then, we might look at the idea of gun control, down the line, as more of a possible solution to the crime problem in society," I replied.

I distributed the project assignment (figure 1), which included my expectations and the rubric for the project. I then gave them time to study it so that they could get an idea of what they were in for—hopefully, they would select an issue that truly interested them.

Workshop Time

I arranged the class into workshops for the remainder of the quarter. Because this type of project required so many different types of work, the students needed the opportunity to do many things while I was available to facilitate and guide. Sean and Jim, for example, were having difficulty locating articles on the diminishing rain forests and expected to have the same trouble finding experts to interview. The workshop format provided me with the opportunity to go off to the English office with them and research the telephone numbers of agencies they might wish to call.

When they returned to class, I asked what they had found out. Their enthusiasm was obvious. They talked to "some guy" who wanted to send them all sorts of "stuff" on the rain forest. These two students had been passive participants in class all year as we studied literature and tried to learn some new writing skills. Suddenly, finding themselves in charge of this project, needing to communicate with "real people" out in their community, they were excited and committed, and they wanted to share what they had learned with others who were also working on the rain forest topic. We began to have informal groups on workshop days, the groups arranged according to issues, so that students could draw on each other's methods and findings.

In these groups, I was able to observe many fascinating transformations and transactions. Students wanted to know if they could work together to develop one survey for use by everyone. "What would the advantage of that be?" I asked them. "We could get more ideas and organize our efforts to interview more people," they replied. I began to regard the momentum of this project with a certain awe; it was my first year of teaching, and before my eyes, I was watching things I had studied in education classes come to life. Some groups

---

Social Problems: Project Assignment

There are many significant social problems worth examining. In this study, you will choose some particular aspect of a problem. Given the environmental crisis, for example, you might explore the problem of waste disposal. Or you might research and write about the rain forests. Ideally, you will choose a topic that both interests and concerns you, one you truly care about! However, you might choose a problem that is unfamiliar, that you do not understand. Homelessness might be an example. In any case, keep an open, questioning mind. Challenge your own attitudes and expectations. Be willing to learn about something so you can know the truth. You will be, in essence, an investigative reporter.

You will conduct the following activities, including the preparation of a final paper:

1. *Survey/Interview.* You will compose a survey or a series of interview questions. You will interview an expert in the field, or you will poll at least five people. Your completed surveys or your summary of the interview will be turned in for credit.

2. *Reading.* You will search for and read several primary sources: newspaper articles, magazine articles, books that report on direct experience with the problem. Summaries of these will be submitted for credit in the course of preparing your paper.

3. *Opinion Letter.* You will compose a letter to a responsible public official, the editor of a newspaper, or some other appropriate recipient, expressing your opinions about your subject.

4. *Written Report.* The resulting paper will be typed. There is no formal requirement for number of pages, but a thorough paper that will earn a distinguished grade will likely be ten or more pages and meet the following criteria:
   - proofread thoroughly; and
   - demonstrates mastery of writing skills.

5. *Oral Report.* Present an oral summary of your study of this problem to the class.

This is a major project, one that will require your careful, ongoing attention. You will wish to incorporate into your paper the material from your survey/interview and from your reading.

Figure 1. Class project assignment.

elected to use the group-prepared questionnaire; others decided to keep their questionnaires individualized.

We paused on occasion to confer with each other as a class about certain things. The issue of audience loomed large over many projects: "Who are you writing to? Who are you focusing on in your papers?" This is why some students decided to keep their surveys individualized, a few pointed out, because they wanted to focus on different aspects of the problem.

Once they began their research, they submitted a series of progress reports to let me know they were moving ahead, and where exactly they were going. They had to find at least two articles—"No, a three-sentence blurb in the *Oakland Tribune* does *not* constitute an article," I pointed out to one or two—and produce a summary that contained three identifiable main points which they would stress in their papers. Armed with the article and the upcoming interviews and surveys, they began to develop their papers. I did not give them any strict format for the paper; instead, we brainstormed and came up with the criteria for an effective, thorough paper. I typed up their ideas, added mine, and gave them everything in handout form the next day (figure 2).

They followed the same procedure with their interviews and surveys: summarize findings, identify several main points to use in their papers. When it came to the interviews and questionnaires, we spent time going over the mechanics of the process, looking at sample interviews and questionnaires, as well as the appropriate etiquette. One obvious outcome of this small part of the assignment was that the students learned to draw information from many sources and to incorporate it into one paper to support a larger idea. Another was that they learned how to interact with people in a variety of situations and how to conduct serious discussions about important matters.

Papers in Progress

The students began to put together their findings, interviews, and ideas about what *they* thought about the subject. After nearly a month of work, I was not hearing any complaints, and I had witnessed some fine work by some previously unenthusiastic members of the class. By this point, most, but not all, were ready to get down to some draft writing. So, cooperating with Joanne, the teacher who heads the computer lab, the students began going to the lab on workshop days to write their papers. Thus, the workshop continued to provide the flexibility needed for adapting to new and changing directions in the project.

As the project progressed, I began to detect a different tone and maturity in many of my students. Suddenly, they were becoming aware of problems that concerned them, that were significant, and that they realized they could do something about. This last realization

---

Social Problems: Outline for Paper

Here are some suggestions and guidelines for your written report. Not all suggestions will apply to all papers.

Introduction: Statement of Problem
- Background on the problem (when it was recognized, who it involved, definitions).
- Causes of the problem.
- Show it. Use your skills to illustrate your problem with graphics, art, tables, and charts so that we can see a polluted river, where a homeless person sleeps, the rain forest being cut.

Discussion of the Problem
- Present the impact on the environment, society, individuals, animals, etc.
- Contributing factors.
- Human impact.
- Costs.

Past and Present Solutions
- What has been done through government and private programs, individual efforts.
- What did or did not work? Why? Is it still being tried? If so, why or why not?

Proposed Solution
- What else might be tried? What would be necessary to try it? Compare these to what has been done.

Conclusion
- How does this problem fit into the "big picture"? Is there any hope?
- What is the individual's responsibility?
- What do you want us to remember about your study?

Figure 2. Outline for brainstorming the paper.

was especially important, for in studying problems of this magnitude, one can become overwhelmed easily by feelings of helplessness. After plugging into such organizations as Greenpeace, Rain Forest Action Network, local homeless agencies, and other associations, the students' potential fears began to abate because they learned what *could* be done. The experience therefore became one of civic involvement and empowerment.

Their empowerment was bolstered further by the next step. Once they had pulled all their facts together and begun to write their papers, the students felt well enough informed to write at least one letter, so I sent a group of them to the library to locate and gather the addresses of our local, state, and federal politicians. They all wrote letters to these representatives (or some other appropriate authority) and in the process, they were learning that writing has a useful purpose in the real world, that they can have a say in things that affect their lives.

Meanwhile, their notion of a community was expanding daily. They were no longer safely hidden away in this little bedroom community with one high school; they were writing to Washington, D.C., about situations in South America; to Sacramento about hunger in Los Angeles; to local politicians about homelessness in the Bay Area. And as their research continued, they were able to offer solutions, and not just simple ones, but significant proposals, citing reputable and irrefutable sources from magazines, newspapers, and expert testimony. Some female students who had once spent the entire period trying to sneak a quick look at their pocket mirrors were now coming to me on Monday and telling me that when they went shopping in San Francisco over the weekend, they saw some homeless families and talked to them before they went into a store to buy their new prom dresses. One or two even told me that they felt uncomfortable about going into the store after seeing or talking with homeless persons. This was not necessarily what I wanted, but it did show a developing social conscience concerned with the world and the people in it.

The Final Stretch

As they moved into the final stages of their papers, the students continued with their workshop groups, using them for editing and peer-response. The groups served an important function: because all of them were informed about the process, they made educated, helpful responders when they looked at each other's papers. They also saw how, for instance, Shannon, one of the most capable students in the class, approached a particular problem that many of them had found difficult to handle. They learned from each other and began to confirm a suspicion I have long had: the harder and longer people work at something, the more important it becomes to them.

As the end of the quarter neared, they had only one more task ahead of them before turning in their papers. Our sophomore classes require an ongoing public speaking emphasis, so the students presented their papers to the class. It was like a convention of scientists, social scientists, and social workers; they sat attentively and listened as each person stood up and presented his or her findings, altogether an amazing array of topics—from transportation to waste disposal, greenhouse effect to AIDS. And as each student stepped down from the front of the class, a place where I had stood very little during the past quarter, the class broke into thunderous applause.

Finally, the last day arrived. I called the students up, one at a time, and checked off their papers, putting a little mark next to their names to assure myself and them that their papers were turned in. Saddled with this much work and such large projects, I did not want anyone to be able to tell me that he or she had turned in a paper but have no way to prove it. One by one, they walked up with their neatly folded papers, nearly every one of them over ten typed pages— a length they nearly had a heart attack over when I first outlined the project—and illustrated with cutout pictures, graphs, or hand-drawn illustrations to clarify their points. They dropped the folders into the box in front of me and smiled with pride and satisfaction at the substantial "thud" which the weight of the paper made in the box.

When all the papers were turned in, the class sighed, almost in unison—the sigh of satisfaction that comes after hard work, real work, not the sigh of "Thank God that's over." It was the sigh of having done what they could do about a problem, one they had come to care about—a sound that I imagined them giving off again and again in the future, as they realized that they were members of a community much larger than Castro Valley, or even the United States. It was the sound I hoped they would make in future years, after they walked out of the voting booth or after they put a letter in the postbox to a politician, having asserted themselves as citizens.

7 Objectivity and Prejudice in Writing about AIDS

Gerald F. Luboff
County College of Morris, Randolph, New Jersey

Research studies and personal experience have shown that college students seem to lack a concrete knowledge about AIDS; particularly, they misunderstand the means of transmission. Many also display stereotypical thinking about the roles which homosexuals and IV drug users play in the transmission of the disease. These facts prompted me to have my freshman students confront and examine their own feelings toward and understanding of AIDS, as well as the issues raised by its existence. I decided to apply the "Three R's: Research, Reaction, and Rhetorical Approaches" to the assignments given in my composition class, using these methods to determine and explore the attitudes of my students, attitudes which I expected would reveal both objectivity and prejudice.

The first assignment involved an exploration of misconceptions about AIDS. To begin, the students had to do some research in approaching the assignment. Specifically, they were asked to find a recent article (one that appeared within the past year) in a newspaper or magazine which disputed two commonly held notions that they—or those they knew—had about AIDS. In addition, since they were to concern themselves with misconceptions, it was obvious that they would be using the rhetorical approach of comparison and contrast, this to be done in the usual 500-word theme.

There were approximately ninety students involved in this assignment, and I was pleased to see that the papers revealed no virulent prejudices, only garden-variety ones, toward homosexuals. For example, both John and Michelle believed that AIDS was a disease contracted only by drug users and homosexuals. Vicki believed that only *gay men*, not *gay women*, could contract the virus. Sergio, in fact, believed that "gays automatically got the virus."

However, I found that my students learned, through their research, that knowledge about the disease eliminated both prejudices and misconceptions: for example, that even casual contact with an infected individual (i.e., sitting next to that person in class) could cause one to become infected; that AIDS is really a problem only of the inner cities, not the suburbs or rural areas; that a heterosexual teenager could not become infected; or that if one were to become infected, AZT was a guaranteed, automatic cure.

Assignment number two involved writing about some controversial aspect of the AIDS crisis. We spent a full class period raising issues and concerns, ultimately narrowing the areas under discussion into workable topics and questions. For example, should someone who has tested positive for the HIV virus be required to carry an ID card to that effect? Should someone in the medical profession who has tested positive be allowed to continue his or her practice? Should husbands or wives who have tested positive be allowed to have children?

In writing their papers, they had to incorporate five of the eighteen terms listed below:

innocent	quarantine	heterosexual	safe
guilty	victim	acceptance	anger
disease	compassion	rejection	unsafe
understanding	outcast	gay	
prevention	homosexual	straight	

Each of these terms carries some kind of emotional weight, so I was interested to see *which* words would be most frequently chosen and *how* those words would be used. The words used most frequently by the students were *disease*, *victim*, and *prevention* (each fifteen times or more), yet none of the words in the list was used in association with prejudicial attitudes. In fact, just about everyone exhibited an understanding of the problems and showed compassion toward those who had been infected with the HIV virus—a very positive but unexpected discovery on my part!

In her paper on AIDS testing in the workplace, Diana noted that, as a result of the sometimes vague and inconclusive testing methods, "An *innocent* person can appear *guilty* and thus be discriminated against." Another student, however, in a well-written paper which presented a strong argument against allowing doctors who test positive to continue their medical practice, *did* perhaps reveal a subconscious prejudice toward gays: he understood the plight of the doctors, he stated, "whether they contracted the virus through *infected* needles or *homosexual* contact"; yet, he never suggested the possibility of their having contracted the disease through heterosexual contact, though *heterosexual* was a word that he might have selected from the list.

The final assignment was a reaction paper. This piece was the most successful of the three. Instructions concerning the assignment (figure 1) were passed out to the classes just before they saw the film *Imagine This,* an eighteen-minute documentary (produced and directed in 1989 by Laurie Vollen, M.D.) featuring interviews with a number of college students (gay, straight, and bisexual) who had been infected with the HIV virus. After viewing the film, the students were asked to write their paper at once.

What I found was that in the majority of cases, the initial reaction was anger, followed by compassion for people with AIDS. However, the anger was multidirectional: sometimes it was directed toward the people with AIDS themselves, if it was discovered that they had not used proper precautions during sexual intercourse or if they were IV drug users; sometimes it was directed toward a capricious universe that allowed this disease to exist; sometimes it was directed specifically toward God for permitting this to happen—both to a specific individual and to society in general.

In most cases, however, the students were compassionate and stated that they would not abandon friends or relatives who contracted the disease. Nevertheless, perhaps because the students were not given time to "adjust" their initial reactions, or because they had to think about the AIDS crisis in terms of individual people rather than society in general, some prejudices did surface. A number of students, for example, still felt that one could contract AIDS through casual contact— they did not believe the doctors or those in public health who stated to the contrary—and therefore wanted to avoid anyone who had tested positive for the AIDS virus. A few students, who were otherwise sympathetic toward "innocent" victims of AIDS, stated that those who share needles for drug use "almost deserve to get AIDS." Only one student directed his anger specifically toward the homosexual community, stating that gays "by rights deserve to get AIDS." He added that only "one guy in the film looked 'normal'"; ironically, this individual was a gay, not straight, male. This student, in fact, refused to complete the second part of the assignment because he found the subject distasteful, could not imagine ever knowing someone who had AIDS, and maintained that he was "by no means a homosexual."

Reaction Paper

The film you are about to see deals with real people, not with characters in a short story, novel, or play. All are involved with a global, yet personal, situation; and they are very aware of what they want to say and of how they feel. In an approximately 300–350-word paper, one that is well organized and clearly presented, first discuss your reaction to these people—or to any one of them—and the problem they face. Second, broaden the situation to include a reaction to the following hypothetical case: You have just discovered that a member of your immediate family, or a boyfriend or girlfriend, best friend, the person sitting next to you in class, or a close coworker faces the same problem. Your reaction may be objective or emotional. The important thing, however, is to express yourself honestly about both situations.

Figure 1. Guidelines for reaction-paper assignment.

On the whole, these writing exercises were beneficial because they not only gave the students the opportunity to practice various rhetorical approaches, they also provided them the opportunity to explore their own attitudes toward the problems and issues raised by the AIDS crisis, and to deal more openly with their prejudices.

8 Introducing Gay and Lesbian Issues in Freshman Composition

Thomas Dukes
University of Akron

With the increased recognition that the college or university community is, in fact, many communities, a number of us have tried to make our students aware of these differences (see Bleich 1989; Berg et al. 1989). This work is not at all unlike that of the archetypal schoolmarm on the frontier, seeking to teach basic math and literacy skills; those of us teaching multiculturalism are simply teaching for a new literacy, a new kind of cultural literacy, albeit a somewhat different one than that imagined by E. D. Hirsch.

At institutions similar to the University of Akron, one is apt to come across considerable student resistance to this process (see, for example, Bogdan 1990). For example, although many students would pay lip service to the idea of "equal pay for equal work," many other elements of feminism (choice issues, the patriarchal foundation of Western religion, etc.) cause the indicator on the student resistance meter to rise appreciably, to say the least. In matters of race, students have been fairly well indoctrinated that it is perhaps bad manners to make racist statements, but this teaching only has the effect of stifling debate, except when the subject is affirmative action; then the indicator jumps on the student resistance meter, even higher than with many feminist issues. If this student resistance, confusion, and even anger can be channeled into writing, we can all benefit; if not, the end result is simply student belief that the professor is (groan) a liberal and that students should write only what the professor wants to hear.

The first time I tried to bring up gay and lesbian issues in a writing class, the indicator on my student resistance meter simply went off the chart. In the fifteen years I have been teaching, nothing ever quite received the response given to my presentation of a story from the campus newspaper about "The Rock." In response to chalk-drawn, pink triangles on university sidewalks, several university students had painted various homophobic words and statements on the oft-used rock; then they proudly posed for a campus newspaper photographer who happened by at the moment. The ensuing controversy caused strong reaction in my writing class, much of which I found deeply disturbing. Yet, when I tried, in as civil and understanding a manner as possible, to question my students about their attitudes, they responded with raised eyebrows or the cold silence students use when confronted with yet another professor they think of as an oppressor.

I decided then to include a segment on gay and lesbian issues in my honors-level writing course on contemporary issues (and I have since done so in "regular" composition classes as well). The problem was doing this in such a way that I did not stifle student writing. At the same time, I did not want to encourage a series of mindless papers full of stereotypical statements about sin and nature. (Don't misunderstand; I am in favor of free speech, and I realize those attitudes reflect student thinking. I simply do not want my students to write— or me to read, evaluate, and grade—uncritical and uninformed discussions.)

My purpose was not to turn my University of Akron freshmen into gay liberationists, an unlikely prospect in any event, but rather to get them to think through their writing about one of the more difficult and explosive social issues of their day. I have often motivated students to write about feminism in interesting ways, because some of the women in each class would challenge the complacency of the other students; I frequently inspire both African American and Anglo-American students to write effectively about race, when they discover that the idealism taught to them about race relations is in conflict with their own observations and experiences. In other words, I could get them thinking on the page about their own, often ambiguous feelings regarding these and other social issues. Could I not do the same about gay and lesbian issues?

My first hurdle was their antipathy toward the subject. If I simply mentioned the topic, I heard giggles, contemptuous snorts, or the silence of the withdrawing student whose attitude is "please let it end." What follows in this essay is a suggested course of action for introducing gay and lesbian issues into the freshman writing class, without raising student hackles to such a degree that learning and writing become impossible. I have constructed this approach from trial and error in my own classes. These techniques were more successful in some classes than in others; some students were so reluctant that

I never got past the first one or two stages in the process. Nor do I mean to suggest that this methodology eliminates homophobic thinking or writing; I can no more wipe that out in an entire freshman class than I can eliminate diction errors and the "it's" problem. But I do mean to suggest that homophobia among students can be addressed through writing—their own and that of other writers, as well.

First, I decided to approach the matter obliquely through another subject. I chose a passage from Garrett Keizer's marvelous book about teaching high school in rural Vermont, *No Place But Here* (1988), in which he has a lovely chapter called "Sex and Faith." Keizer discusses how our young people are taught coarse attitudes about sex and about each other:

> Without mentioning a name, I tell them [his students] of a gay student I had, tall and strong—"you wouldn't have gotten away with calling him a sissy." And I think to myself of his letter; at the time he was stationed near San Francisco—"not minding the Service at all"—and would soon be sailing north to "someplace called the Illusion Islands." Like most of us, gay or straight, male or female, he will find his illusions chillier than expected, but I wish him well in his life, and I say so out loud to the class.
>
> I do not as yet say anything about the courage, the compassion, and the suffering of another boy—short and frail this time—who hated nothing in his life so much as being a boy. But how I wish some of my students could have sat in on our first conference, which he requested only hours after I had lectured in Bible as Literature on "The Parables and the Outcasts," and have heard some of what it means, not to be one in ten, but to be one in hundreds of thousands. I wish they [the students] and their parents, too, could have read his final exam, where he discusses the words of Jesus telling his disciples to love their enemies, and yet to shake from their feet the dust of a town that rejects them. (37–38)

This backdoor approach is effective for several reasons. First, the subject of the chapter is high school and the way teenagers are taught, not just in school, but in the larger culture. Freshmen are quite responsive to this subject; for many of these students, high school has been their most important community experience thus far. Second, the voice, the persona, of the chapter belongs to a man who sounds like the perfect teacher; students respond favorably to that.

Of course, what makes the chapter, as a whole, and the particular excerpt I quoted so ideal is that this perfect teacher leads the students to consider the gay and the transsexual student, possibly someone sitting next to them, as having sexual struggles just as significant as their own, something Keizer also discusses in the chapter. And the author discusses these students and sex in terms of a religious figure, namely Jesus Christ, that many of my students have at least been taught to respect, if not to worship.

My class goes on to discuss the voice of the writer and the role of the teacher here, but most important, we discuss, as readers, our written responses to the two quoted paragraphs, how we make meaning from them, what is our own enculturation about the topic, and so on. I have students *anonymously* freewrite response statements—two paragraphs at most—to the passage I have quoted. I then read the statements out loud; they may range from the most homophobic, to the veiled "I-*am*-that-guy-in-the-paragraph." Student writing thus forms the basis of our discussion; my students create their own texts, which they must then respond to and for which we as a class must account.

One key element here is that students feel safer discussing their own prejudices and attitudes in a group. Another, for me as a writing teacher, is that students see how writing and thinking connect. My next step often has students writing response statements to our discussion. What has usually happened is that the strongest homophobia begins to turn to something on the order of well-okay-but-I-don't-want-that-queer-and-that-weirdo-near-me. I have no illusions about causing attitudinal reversals as a result of our discussion and writing, but I am able to demonstrate how thinking about the issue through writing, talking about our writing, discussing how writing affected our thoughts and vice versa has enabled us to reformulate our thoughts about the subject of our discussion. Undeniably, a great deal of homophobia may be aired in discussion and writing; nonetheless, students are involved in thinking about and revising their attitudes and judgments.

As my students write, we also discuss the language of homosexuality, specifically words such as "queer," "dyke," and "faggot." Either to trigger discussion or in response to student remarks, I ask students to speculate on the differences between, say, calling a girl a "tomboy" and a boy a "sissy." While this approach and the discussion it generates may seem almost embarrassingly obvious, I have found two surprising (at least to me) results. First, the males in the class say much about the scorn heaped on even the most masculine-acting guys who show a bit of "sissy" behavior, as opposed to the support they believe is given to "tomboy" girls. (I am beginning to think that almost every male has at some time been called a "sissy"; Paul Theroux has a good related essay on male behavior called "Being a Man" [1991].)

The women in the class will often argue that, while adults may find tomboy behavior admirable in girls, other girls often do not. Still other women in the class might say that they were praised from all sides for being "tomboys," while some men will say that it was the intellectual, bookish, even artistic guys who got the adult praise and attention. My point is simply that the class sees how the culture's demand that we conform to certain gender behaviors can create either problems or success, depending on where we fall. Students will often follow this with a discussion of how expected gender behaviors may or may not be changing. Furthermore, they may observe that changes in these expected behaviors have affected straight and gay individuals alike. In another freewriting exercise, I ask the students to speculate about these changes.

To move from freewriting to more formal discourse, I first have students read any one of a number of publications that I bring to class or that are in a text I have chosen for the course. While I am both frustrated and angry that many recent text-readers will include essays on every controversial topic under the sun *except* gay and lesbian life, there are some exceptions (see Stoddard 1989; Allison 1990; Leavitt 1990; Weinberg 1990; Sullivan 1991). In a contemporary issues class, for instance, any essay that deals intelligently with AIDS works well if it discusses the disease within the context of gay life. One might also show either a part or all of the movie *Desert Hearts* or the recent television program *Oranges Are Not the Only Fruit* to discuss lesbian concerns. Student response to these materials is as varied as you might expect, but these essays and programs provide excellent stimuli to which students may choose to respond in their more formal response papers.

For their formal papers, then, I let students choose whether to write a response statement to our class discussion or to the reading or movie watching we have done in class. Their doing so depends, of course, on their having taken careful notes and, more important, on their trust in the instructor. These papers generally indicate that students are struggling with complex feelings about their own sexuality. Some students admit to being threatened or "turned off" by gays or lesbians; others will repeat the clichés and outright falsehoods they have heard while growing up. In my evaluations of these papers, I will often write many questions in the margins and correct outright untruths— for example, that homosexual men are predisposed to be child molesters or that all lesbians either truly hate men or truly want one—but I never grade down a student for writing uninformed prejudices or demonstrably false statements.

I realize that many of the students in class are exploring what, for them, is very dangerous territory, so I confine my grading to organization, coherence, and the usual grammar and mechanics. I do not even work that much on voice, here, except to encourage students to be frank about their own uncertainties and questions; as a result, I think students feel free to admit their own confusions about gay and lesbian sexuality. Because I am aware of how uncomfortable some of them are with these subjects, I have also let students avoid writing a formal paper about these issues by allowing them to write on a related topic.

This is the point where I must say something about my own presence in the classroom. In a marvelous essay from *College English,* Dale Bauer (1990) discusses "The Other 'F' Word: Feminist in the Classroom." Following Charles Paine, Bauer says we must "accept our own roles as rhetoricians" (368), and she goes on to argue "that political commitment—especially feminist commitment—is [for her] a legitimate classroom strategy and rhetorical imperative" (389). Bauer agrees with Pat Bizzell that we challenge students' foundational beliefs, and Bauer believes it is perfectly legitimate to offer feminism as a foundational belief for students (390). As you might expect, Bauer and her like-minded colleagues receive a great deal of student resistance in this process; we ask students "to give allegiance to an affinity or coalition politics that often competes with or negates other allegiances they have already formed" (391). Yet, Bauer believes that her feminism and commitment to social change require her to challenge her students and, paradoxically, require them to express their own doubts about her position in the class (391).

For my students, at least, I believe a somewhat different position is called for. I have decided that a direct discussion about my own sexual identity is not required or even appropriate. This decision is based on my role as a rhetorician; activism on my part, beyond what I have described in this paper, would come between the larger dialogue in which my class and I engage, as well as between my students and their writing and, in some instances, my students' trust in me and their faith in my ability to judge their writing with what they believe is "objectivity." My judgments as a rhetorician have led me to include this unit smack in the middle of the semester, at a point where my students believe they can trust me with their writing and their ideas;

I do not want to do anything that will diminish that trust. Therefore, if, in the classroom, I am not to homosexuality what Dale Bauer is to feminism, I would claim that my rhetorical approach is not merely the best that can be expected, given student attitudes and expectations; rather, my approach is the best rhetorical stance in the classroom for an instructor who aims to challenge and teach, not stifle and frighten.

More important, my goal is to get students to write, and even if they write homophobic papers, they begin to analyze their own thinking through writing, and that, I contend, should be one of the principal goals of any writing class. While I am frustrated at not always being able to change minds, I have introduced students to the topic of homosexuality and made them aware that gay men and lesbian women are very much a part of the culture in which the students find themselves. That introduction and the student writing which follows it constitute a major accomplishment for both instructor and student, an important first step in educating our students as to the variety of people who make up the community in which they will live and work.

Works Cited

Allison, Dorothy. 1990. "Don't Tell Me You Don't Know." In McQuade and Atwan, 219–30.

Bauer, Dale. 1990. "The Other 'F' Word: Feminist in the Classroom." *College English* 52: 385–96.

Berg, Allison, et al. 1989. "Breaking the Silence: Sexual Preference in the Composition Classroom." *Feminist Teacher* 4. 2–3: 29–32.

Bleich, David. 1989. "Homophobia and Sexism as Popular Values." *Feminist Teacher* 4. 2–3: 21–28.

Bogdan, Deanne. 1990. "Censorship, Identification, and the Poetics of Need." In *The Right to Literacy*, edited by Andrea Lunsford et al., 128–47. New York: MLA.

Keizer, Garret. 1988. *No Place But Here*. New York: Viking.

Leavitt, David. 1990. "Territory." In McQuade and Atwan, 203–19.

McQuade, Donald, and Robert Atwan, eds. 1990. *The Winchester Reader*. Boston: Bedford.

Stoddard, Thomas B. 1989. "Gay Marriages: Make Them Legal." In *Current Issues and Enduring Questions: Methods and Models of Argument*, edited by Sylvan Barnet and Hugo Bedau, 45–47. Boston: Bedford.

Sullivan, Andrew. 1991. "Here Comes the Groom." In *Elements of Argument: A Text and Reader*, 3rd ed., edited by Annette Rottenberg, 164–68. Boston: Bedford.

Theroux, Paul. 1991. "Being a Man." In *The Longwood Reader,* edited by Edward A. Dornan and Charles W. Dawe, 468–73. Boston: Allyn and Bacon.

Weinberg, George. 1990. "The Madness and Myths of Homophobia." In McQuade and Atwan, 196–203.

III Acquiring a Taste for Literature

English teachers are serious about their students' experiences with literature. They desire for their students the same positive, enriching encounters with drama, story, novel, biography, and poem that they had. Therefore, they are ever vigilant for approaches that improve the meeting between literature and students, for selections and methods that maximize students' appreciation, personal growth, and intellectual understanding.

English teachers seek to move students beyond the nuts and bolts of literary invention to an application of ideas and values from literature to their own lives. Involvement, motivation, seriousness, and introspection therefore become keys in successful programs.

Here, we benefit from the practices of teachers who have dared to break out from the formulaic literature lesson by designing ways for students to become active, satisfied readers of valuable literary fare.

Phyllis B. Schwartz "Peel[s] an Onion without Tears" to demonstrate two graphic modes—the literary sociogram and the story location chart—as ways for readers to respond to literature.

In "Toward 'Discussions with Oneself,'" Joanna Schultz takes us on an odyssey from study guides to response journals. Her students' journal entries, written while reading Richard Wilbur's "First Snow in Alsace," provide convincing evidence for the journey.

Daniel D. Victor describes a two-level evolution in his literature class, as students trace the change in a single author's work over time while the teacher moves the class well beyond the read-discuss-test mode of the traditional anthology.

In his "Walk on a Rainbow Trail," Joel Kammer shows us why he uses works by popular mystery writer Tony Hillerman in his classroom. He demonstrates how Hillerman's *Skinwalkers* can provide high school seniors with an intensive reading experience.

Two teachers offer ways to make a Shakespeare play accessible and vital to high school students. Elise Ann Earthman, in "Teaching Shakespeare in the Inner City," makes *Macbeth* a successful experience for students at Mission High School by applying response theory, a very thorough preparation beforehand, and an acting perspective. Carol Meinhardt "Offer[s] Literature with Respectful Deception," luring her tenth graders into a meaningful encounter with *Romeo and Juliet.*

Applying a collaborative learning approach, JoAnna Stephens Mink provides her college students with a significant, involved learning experience in dramatic literature in "The Collaborative Term Paper."

In "Connecting with the Classics," Barbara Jones Brough has her students play back and forth between classic literary pieces and contemporary culture, making linkages that construct meaning for the literature and that develop literary applications for their modern lives.

Perry Oldham demonstrates the importance of experiencing poetry before analyzing it, and goes on to show students carrying out "experiential" presentations for their classmates, in "On Teaching Poetry."

Gary Watson describes a way to apply nineteenth-century American thinking to contemporary political circumstances by having "Transcendentalists Run for President."

9 Peeling an Onion without Tears

Phyllis B. Schwartz
Lord Byng Secondary School, Vancouver, British Columbia

Generating teenage enthusiasm for literary essay writing is no easy feat. Perhaps because academic literary topics are remote from the urgency of their lives, or because they doubt their ability to make meaning from what they read, many young writers carry poor self-images of themselves as students in an English class. I have always found it a joy, therefore, to liberate them from this negative self-perception with its resulting literary paralysis. Sometimes all it takes to build their confidence is a new trick or device—one that helps students tap into the wellspring of their own minds, one that frees up a wealth of knowledge and confidence they can apply to literature assignments.

Methods derived from Louise Rosenblatt, James Moffett, and Nancie Atwell can serve to engage students in literary thinking. What follows are student-centered methods that aid maturing readers as they find their way into sound literary analysis and prewriting. These strategies can yield refreshing insights that lead to well-founded literature essays. Beginning with some of the basic tenets of reader-response theory, students analyze literature via two strategies: literary sociograms and location charts. Both of these activities are frameworks for thinking that yield data for analysis and a structure for subsequent writing about literature.

The *reader-response* approach to teaching literature is an open-ended reading process. Students bring to the text their prior knowledge, attitudes, and previous reading experiences. On the basis of their initial reactions, the teacher can orchestrate learning experiences that allow students to engage in literary study appropriate to their needs and interests. This begins with personal reaction to a text—the end product of which cannot always be predicted or controlled—and requires several conditions if it is to be successful and effective.

Students need to understand that they are actively engaged participants, not passive observers. The meaning of the text emerges as they identify places in the text that *are* engaging. At first, the meaning is tentative, but as these initial meanings are explored and shared, the reader can go deeper by returning to the text, connecting personal experience, prior knowledge, and shared meaning. While the direction of the meaning comes from the students, the rules for this process require that they continually return to the text for verification and support. A climate of trust is needed if students are to respond personally to text and accept a meaning that is initially tentative. The teacher must be prepared to guide students through this process, understanding that there are no fixed or standard answers. For significant literary thinking, talking, and writing, students and the teacher need reading materials that are equally worthy of this type of reflection. This process is much like peeling layers off an onion in order to get to the center.

Instead of identifying plot, character, setting, and theme as starting points, students are asked to write about connecting points in literature that awaken or arrest them. These responses could be categorized as thematic responses, character development responses, plot development responses, and the like. But more commonly, these meanings begin with response journals in which students write about significant passages or events. Sometimes meanings are deepened by comparing elements in literature to elements in their own lives. By writing about a parallel experience, students are exploring both literature and their own experience, and often comparison spontaneously yields generalization. Sharing initial responses validates common reactions and invites opportunities for cross-fertilization and defense of positions. To do this, students return to the text and the cycle repeats.

Many of the activities in the English class engage a student's linguistic intelligence; that is, they ask the student to play with language—decode print materials in writing and conversations, manipulate one's own words on paper, retell stories in one's own words. For some students, this is quite difficult, but if asked to use their spatial intelligence, they find *representing* their responses in graphic form a natural expression of their thinking process. When students represent ideas in media such as graphics, illustrations, puppetry, role-playing, diagrams, plot graphs, and the like, they are manipulating symbols and working with extended metaphors.

What follows are two forms for representing responses to literature that use graphic and iconic representation. By using the elements of graphics, structure is given to both student thought and the written assignment. The first, the *literary sociogram*, provides opportunities to analyze the human relationships within a piece of literature. The second, the *location chart,* engages students in the pursuit of thematic elements that reside in a location within a literary event. Both are foundation activities for generalizing and making hypotheses about the meanings of texts.

Literary Sociograms

Sociologists use sociograms to study the relationships between people in groups and communities. In a diagram, one can view the relationships between people within a group. These relationships are connected with arrows that show one-way and mutual relationships; a boomerang arrow shows an influence that brings about a change after contact (figure 1). This process, applied to the study of literature, can provide students with the opportunity to visualize graphically the relationships within a story; the technique can be extended to demonstrate relationships between characters, events, background, and other relevant literary elements present in the literature. Some of my students, for example, used this process to diagram relationships in *Oedipus Rex, King Lear, Pygmalion,* and *Shoeless Joe.*

Introducing the technique of making a literary sociogram can be done by taking a commonly known fairy tale and using the sociogram to demonstrate its construction. As a class activity, the teacher can use the overhead and ask students to direct the placement of characters, to name the lines, and to locate regions. The basic task is to use arrows to diagram the relationships between characters and between items that bring about change within the story (figure 1). The name on each arrow is essential because it defines the relationship. In class discussion, my students debated locations for characters, regions of the story, and names of the lines describing relationships between characters and symbols. After items were laid out, the students were asked to connect these characters and items by using the three types of connecting arrows.

Once they practiced it, the students were ready to apply this analytical technique to their own reading selections. They were asked to list elements that remained strong in their memory: characters, events, and symbols. Their first task was to represent story elements in two-dimensional form and then place these elements significantly on the page. Next, they were to name relationships. Some used symbols to represent ideas or values. Some students wished to begin using color at this stage; others included color in a revision of their sociogram.

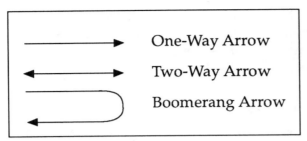

Figure 1. Arrows used in a sociogram.

In the case of *King Lear* (figure 2), students began by answering questions such as, "Where is Lear's name best placed on the page? Is he above, or below, or next to his daughters?" As their sociograms emerged, students connected the following elements:

One-Way Arrows

Lear feels friendship toward Kent; Kent feels loyalty to Lear.

Cordelia is betrayed by her sisters; they feel indifferent toward her.

Both Goneril and Regan envy King Lear.

Two-Way Arrows

Gloucester and Lear experience a mutual friendship.

Goneril and Regan use each other.

Boomerang Arrows

Lear is betrayed by both Goneril and Regan and is changed as a result of this relationship.

Lear and the fool change roles on several occasions throughout the play, and as a result, both are changed by the relationship.

In using sociograms, the following, general questions can help students to focus their work:

Why are items placed where they are placed?

Why did you choose that type of arrow to connect these items?

What word or phrase names the relationship identified by the arrow?

Are there regions forming on your paper? Name them.

Are there time zones forming on your sociogram? Name them.

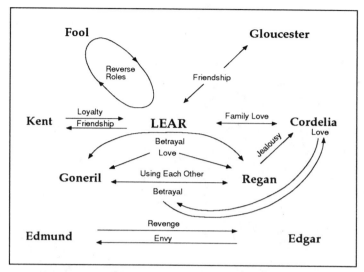

Figure 2. Literary sociogram of *King Lear.* (Courtesy of Simon Stanlake and used with his permission.)

The technique of constructing a literary sociogram provides opportunities for small-group discussion. Using sociograms to diagram and name relationships can be an end in itself: it accesses the dynamics of literature. As a prewriting activity, this method provides structure to a class discussion or an oral presentation. Using overhead transparencies prepared by individuals and groups can stimulate discussions that return readers to the text for validation and further extension. Quotes from the text can also be incorporated, as in the iconographic representation of key quotes from W. P. Kinsella's *Shoeless Joe,* shown in figure 3.

The process of sociogram construction involves both metaphorical thinking and understanding. The diagram of *Shoeless Joe* is not purely a sociogram, because more emphasis is placed on the relationship between key quotes than between characters, and the lines are not named, as well. The diagram, as it is, represents students who were "stuck" because they found three key quotes in the novel and tried to use the baseball diamond metaphor as a model to connect the quotes; the baseball diamond, however, has four bases, technically, and the students could not find a fourth significant quote. However, the students extended this activity by asking questions: "Who ran the

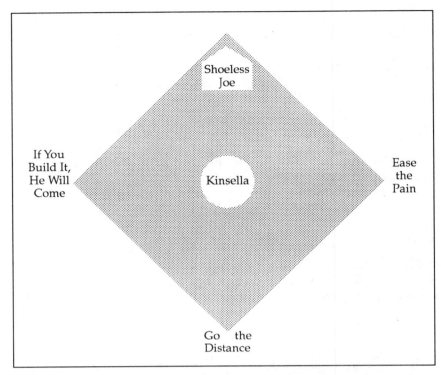

Figure 3. Iconographic representation of key quotes from *Shoeless Joe*.

bases? Who was the pitcher? Did anyone hit a home run?" In an attempt to further and tighten this iconographic representation, another student added "diamonds are forever," and changed the diagram so that it resembled a stylized, faceted diamond. The students who engaged in this literary discussion were secure with tentative thinking as they returned to the text to find evidence for their models and to manipulate symbols and extend metaphors.

After two days, students returned to response writing, and exciting literary essays emerged. Some essays began by explaining some of the sociograms generated by individuals and groups. Others supported their hypotheses with diagrams, sociograms, and conceptual models of their literary interpretations. In the end, students shared exciting, sophisticated, original literary analyses with their classmates.

They were too excited about their original ideas to just submit their papers for marking; instead, they insisted that time be set aside for reading their essays out loud and for sharing their final representations. Their analytical work had been one of peeling off layers of meaning until they arrived at an essential meaning. Their sharing was a celebration of confidence and belief that within themselves as readers were the meanings of the text.

Location Charts

Literary analysis is an intimidating term for many high school students, yet these same students frequently engage in the process of analysis in and out of school. Students analyze their friends, their enemies, their boyfriends and girlfriends, their teachers, and their parents. It is a process that goes hand-in-hand with adolescent development. To build on their strengths and transfer their innate analytical abilities to textual analysis, my students were asked to select pertinent story features for what is known in the film industry as a *location chart.* Without fears or tears, students teased apart texts and, in the analysis of data, found a way into Northrop Frye's archetypal criticism.

To construct a location chart, ask students to imagine that they are filming the short story or novel they have just completed— reminding them that a filmmaker does not shoot a film chronologically, but rather, lists all scenes that take place in one location and plans a shooting schedule. This is an ideal group activity because brainstorming and idea sharing will give students more opportunity to talk about the literature and make critical decisions as they recall events in the story. To enhance this activity, students can be asked to incorporate quotes into the chart. For example, a group of students using this technique while studying *Huckleberry Finn* selected the raft and the shore. The students discovered that the events on the river were extensive, so one student suggested that it would be useful to subdivide the list. Students preparing a location chart of *A Separate Peace* identified the river, the dorm, the town, the playing field, Finny's home, and the hospital. In a debriefing of *The Grapes of Wrath*, students selected the highway, roadside camps, government camps, Oklahoma, and California for their locations, and were in the process of comparing some of these locations to Bible stories before they received the next stage of the assignment. To deepen their use of this data, students were asked controlling questions such as:

What kinds of events take place in each location?

> *Huck Finn:* Huck always gets into mischief on the shore.
>
> *A Separate Peace:* Finny is in charge on the playing field.
>
> *Grapes of Wrath:* Migrant-worker camps form governments.

Identify locations where character change takes place:

> *Huck Finn:* Huck matures on the raft.
>
> *A Separate Peace:* No one is the same after a tree-jump.
>
> *Grapes of Wrath:* Grandparent dies leaving Oklahoma.

What effect does a location have upon a character?

> *Huck Finn:* River—maturity.
>
> *A Separate Peace:* Tree—maturity; see reality.
>
> *Grapes of Wrath:* Camps—build solidarity.

What kind(s) of journey(s) takes place between locations?

Is one location more significant than another? Explain.

Asking students to lay out data graphically provides them with an opportunity to more easily see elements out of chronological order and in an elemental form. Once these examples were generated, students were asked to step back from their location charts and make hypotheses about their data. The student-generated hypotheses surprised everyone, including the students:

- Huck Finn's raft journey was a pure exploration of maturity, and whenever he went on shore, it was tainted by evil and corruption.

- The tree-jump was an initiation into the world of evil and danger, and once the boys jumped, there was no return to the protection of childhood.

- Once families were uprooted from their land in Oklahoma, their bonds were fractured. Their journey to California was a search for new bonds, in hopes that they could grow roots that would again nourish them.

These hypotheses were put on the chalkboards after the students presented their location charts. The boards offered topics for further written exploration, and the location charts contained the detailed data that could support their hypotheses. Next, students were asked to select a hypothesis that attracted them and to expand on it in a response journal. Sharing response journals led to challenging discussions and more cross-fertilization. Students were now ready to write literary essays. Some found the location-chart information useful for developing hypotheses about the relationship between setting and events/characters. Others wrote about the power of the setting. For other students, this exercise was a vehicle for teasing out data that provided opportunities for seeing deeper meaning in the events of the story.

The process had shown them how essay topics are generated. Instead of depending upon the teacher to set a topic, these students had shown themselves how the meaning of the text was within themselves; this, in turn, dictated their writing topics. They had confidence that the next time they read a book, they could come to class with original ideas to contribute to an analytical discussion. The students, at the end of these two exercises, had devices and techniques that would give them a basis for analyzing literature, a basis which came from a source of personal meaning. They had tricks for peeling the literary onion that would help them get to the heart (theirs and the text's) without tears.

Recommended Sources

Atwell, Nancie. 1987. *In the Middle: Writing, Reading, and Learning with Adolescents.* Portsmouth, NH: Boynton/Cook.

Gardner, Howard. 1983. *Frames of the Mind: The Theory of Multiple Intelligences.* New York: Basic Books.

Moffett, James. 1968. *A Student-Centered Language Arts Curriculum, Grades K–13: A Handbook for Teachers.* Boston: Houghton Mifflin.

Rosenblatt, Louise. 1983. *Literature as Exploration.* 3rd ed. New York: MLA.

10 Toward "Discussions with Oneself"

Joanna Schultz
Ellis School, Pittsburgh, Pennsylvania

Five years ago, I defined my mission as a teacher of literature as "helping to initiate students into worlds that are, as yet, foreign to them." My primary teaching method was to assign readings, have students fill in study-guide questions, and then discuss their answers in class. I carefully crafted the study guides so that they encouraged both convergent and divergent thinking, encouraged individual responses to texts, and helped explain the myriad complexities of language that keep students from making meaning of what they read.

During the past few years, though, I have become increasingly uneasy about this teaching strategy. Students claim that having to answer study-guide questions disturbs their reading. Some students simply copy others' answers so they can get through class discussions without revealing that they have not read the book. Class discussions have often been dominated by students seeking the "right" answers to my questions. And the nagging question remains about the concept of "initiating" students. Do I really have the authority to dictate what they will learn from what they read? I am beginning to believe more and more firmly that no teacher should have that authority, and that by attempting to wield it, teachers can narrow and trivialize the responses students will have when making meaning out of texts they read. No matter how good my study-guide questions are, the fact remains that students are filling in my blanks rather than creating their own questions and answers.

A student-centered classroom, where learning about literature is based on free responses to what is being read, would seem to be a solution to my quandary. I would cease being an initiator into the mysteries of literature and would become, instead, a facilitator in students' individual quests. I could see problems, though, in my changing to such a classroom. How would this less-controlled learning experience fit into the curriculum I am supposed to teach? How could

I ensure that my students would engage with the increasingly sophisticated characters and themes they will encounter in their literature course? Would they begin to look at and appreciate the different ways authors put works together to express what they mean? Would my students learn enough?

Reader-response theorists claim that any real meaning we draw from a text is a combination of the intellectual and emotional background we bring to that reading, and the thoughts and feelings of the author that channel it. Accordingly, in order to make meaning, students need direct access to a text, no matter how difficult it may be. Yet the process of studying literature in school, particularly in secondary classrooms, is not often like reading as we know it. Reading is messy and quirky; our insights and pleasure come at unpredictable moments in our search through a text. My study guides are certainly guilty of imposing structures on the act of reading; they change it from a process to be enjoyed to a task with an already-defined result.

Since study guides did not seem the best way to help students evoke true meaning from a text, last year I turned to response journals. In the past, I had used journals as a supplement to study-guide questions. I had asked students to explore connections from their own lives to what they were reading, or I developed exercises which helped them empathize with literary characters. Although I believed that my journal assignments enriched my students' pursuit of literature, I did classify them as enrichment to the real, core learning—that which they did through answering structured questions. In my new student-centered classroom, the journals themselves had to become the core of learning because they were the vehicles for individual responses. The students had less problem with this concept than I did. In her first journal entry last fall, after listening to my explanation of how we were going to use the journals, one student wrote, "I like this. Writing helps me learn about what I don't know about."

Journal responses to literature have many advantages over oral responses. Students gain a sense of empowerment because they have time to formulate responses as well as the opportunity to express them. Early this year, after the reading of a poem, followed by ten minutes of silent journal writing, a student noted, "It was quiet today so I could think. I enjoyed reading a poem and then writing about it so I would be able to have a chance to state my ideas, even if I didn't get called on." The privacy of journals enables all students to have a voice—even the shy ones, the unsure ones, the reflective ones, and the adolescents who have to maintain images contrary to the thoughts and emotions produced through reading.

The process of writing itself has inherent value since it allows students time to reflect, reconsider, and better understand their reactions. A journal writing session often becomes a process of wrestling with confusion, during which students answer their own questions or make surprising discoveries. Trying to solve their own problems may make them read with greater attention. Articulation is developed because response is demanded. A student who writes that a book is boring will be asked to explain what is boring about it, and will be led to discover for herself what she likes or does not like in literature. Journal writing, which is ungraded, also allows students to take the risks and venture the ideas they might have repressed or not even thought of in another type of literature class. My students' wide-ranging responses encompassed every approach that study guides or text questions devised, as well as ones I would never have anticipated.

Written journal entries allow extended teacher-student dialogues to unfold as the teacher responds to each student response. Since the safety of journals allows students to reveal what they do not know, teachers can discover what is not understood. And it is humbling to realize that even the most experienced teachers cannot always anticipate what will confuse or intrigue their students. The teacher individualizes instruction by responding in whatever direction or on whatever level she thinks necessary to extend each student's personal response to literature. Teachers' responses can model thought processes and writing techniques as well as aid in an indirect revision process that does not stifle the students' creativity or freedom. Teachers can also ask questions of students which may lead them into types and levels of responses they have not yet encountered. There is the opportunity here for the real stretching of students' thinking, which I, perhaps falsely, had relied on study guides to provide.

Over the course of the school year, I developed a procedure for the use of response journals in my eighth-grade literature class. If we were reading a poem, essay, or short story, I gave the students copies while I read the work out loud. Then they were asked to reread silently and write a response. I declined to give them directions about what to write. I also insisted that they do nothing else except think and write for that ten to fifteen minutes, in order to discourage the students who write down the first thing they can think of and then claim they have nothing else to say. (The thoughts extracted after a student thinks she is finished are often the most individual and unusual ones she has.) At first, many students asked for more direction about what they should write, but as the year progressed, they became more and more confident in their own powers of observation.

After the students have completed their initial journal response, we can talk. Because each student has had time to develop a response, I can call on anyone to start the discussion, and more students willingly participate than in the past. In fact, discussions often become heated debates between students who are passionately invested in their individual interpretations. Discussion subjects tend to be wide-ranging, and my three sections often discuss entirely different things. Although I am happiest when the students carry the discussion from an examination of one topic to another unassisted, I do participate from time to time by encouraging them to develop the ideas they introduce and by making sure that everyone who wishes to has a chance to speak. Occasionally, when the students run out of ideas, I do initiate another line of discussion, but this has happened less and less frequently. I try to stop discussions about five minutes before the end of the period so that they can write a little more about what they have learned through the discussion. My hope is that this final writing will help them extend the range of their literary responses. It has often done just that, but it has also added a pleasing dimension to this group exploration that I hadn't foreseen. After a journal writing and discussion of one section of Cather's *My Antonia*, one student wrote, "I learned that Caroline [a classmate] really understands people. I'll go to her when I have a problem."

Although the students usually write freely about what they are reading, I occasionally assign journal topics which focus them on an aspect of a literary work or on a kind of response which they might not have thought of themselves. I try to be playful as well as challenging so that they won't stop enjoying their explorations. These assignments also vary the class structure so that we do not get stuck in a rut. Some of last year's topics include the following:

1. Rewriting a scene from another character's point of view. (For *Jane Eyre* and *The Diary of a Young Girl.*)

2. Writing about personal experiences which might lead students into a work. (Reflections on disagreements with parents over independence and authority, leading into a reading of *Romeo and Juliet.*)

3. Responding to one character, one section of a work, or one passage.

4. Exploring what seemed surprising about a work.

5. Predicting what will happen in a work.

6. Finding specific quotations to comment on.

7. Exploring personal feelings on a related topic.

The other writings on literature that my students develop grow out of their journal responses. Last fall, when I assigned a paper topic on *My Antonia,* an assignment which I had developed and used successfully in the past, I met with great resistance. Students objected to leaving their own lines of inquiry to reflect on mine. Subsequent papers, with widely varying topics growing out of their journal responses, have been more interesting, more full of life, and more personal, even if less successful technically than the five-paragraph essays of the past. My hope is that the students' real investment in these papers will encourage them to work on the organization and form necessary for effective communication. I have also had to devise new kinds of tests, since different students and different sections may be learning different things. Essay questions have to be based on class discussions, with some choice included to account for students' different experiences. On each test, I have tried to include questions that allow students to use a personal line of inquiry to discuss the work in question. Even on tests, the process of responding has become more important than the knowledge discovered.

I try to read each student's journal as soon as possible after an entry is written, and I always comment on each response. Although this amount of reading seems intimidating, it is nowhere near as burdensome as reading innumerable essays on the same topic. Through writing, each student develops modes of response and a personality that unfolds as the year progresses. I think I know each student in a new, often deeper way than I have known students in the past. In my comments to students, I answer their questions, ask questions which might further develop a line of inquiry they have started, either make general observations or expand on their observations of specifics in a text, note a particularly unusual or insightful perception, compliment graceful writing, and relate their experiences to ones that I or others have had. I never grade journal entries or criticize a student's thoughts; I am convinced that this would destroy the safe environment of the journals, which allows the kind of risk-taking and struggle that is so important to understanding. With four or five students, I have developed a running correspondence in which we each comment directly on what the other has said. Most students, though, read what I say and then go on to the next project or response.

Journal entries by my eighth-grade students on one of their literary works will demonstrate the range, complexity, and creativity of their responses to literature. They were certainly learning enough! We read Richard Wilbur's poem, "First Snow in Alsace."

First Snow in Alsace*

The snow came down last night like moths
Burned on the moon; it fell till dawn,
Covered the town with simple cloths.

Absolute snow lies rumpled on
What shellbursts scattered and deranged,
Entangled railings, crevassed lawn.

As if it did not know they'd changed,
Snow smoothly clasps the roofs of homes
Fear-gutted, trustless and estranged.

The ration stacks are milky domes;
Across the ammunition pile
The snow has climbed in sparkling combs.

You think: beyond the town a mile
Or two, this snowfall fills the eyes
Of soldiers dead a little while.

Persons and persons in disguise,
Walking the new air white and fine,
Trade glances quick with shared surprise.

At children's windows, heaped, benign,
As always, winter shines the most,
And frost makes marvelous designs.

The night guard coming from his post,
Ten first-snows back in thought, walks slow
And warms him with a boyish boast:

He was the first to see the snow.

—Richard Wilbur

In the past I had used a series of questions designed to lead the students toward a recognition of the poem's tension between the beautiful peace of the year's first snow and the reminders of war buried underneath. My students have had trouble with these questions in the past, making me wonder whether the poem is potentially too

---

difficult, but since it is such a beautiful and troubling poem, I wanted
to try it once more. On January 15, 1991, the day of President Bush's
deadline for Iraq's withdrawal from Kuwait, another try seemed
particularly appropriate.

One student, Janet, used the poem to reflect on the nature of
life from her thirteen-year-old perspective:

> It [the poem] shows how the way an adult sees the first snow
> is so different from the way children see it. Adults have been
> through more things and they know about all the bad things
> in life. . . . The children are carefree and happy, and they're not
> aware of all the fighting around them. They think of snow as
> being beautiful, and they just think that the horrible things
> covered in snow are marvelous designs.

I commented to her that the narrator seems to be caught between
these two worlds. Janet's knowing reply was that "he must not be
much older than me."

Lily, a student who, in the past, had been considerably less able
than Janet, made a subtle distinction between the denotative and
connotative meanings of the words *cold* and *warm:*

> You think of a first snow, and then you think of war which
> gives you a different perspective on it. I think that's why the
> poem has a hint of coldness. But the end is best when it says
> "And warms him with a boyish boast." Snow always makes
> me feel warm.

Lily was not the only student to comment on the use of words, the
subtleties of language which I thought might get lost without my
guidance and prodding. Laura noticed that "the writing was talking
about *war* but did not say the word *war* once." She concluded that
"the poem got the point across better that he was against war than if
he would have just come right out and said it." I have always thought
that I needed to show students the power of imagery! Obviously,
Laura discovered it for herself.

Sally used the reading of "First Snow in Alsace" to help clarify
her views on the world situation:

> I wonder if you gave this to us because of what is happening
> in the Middle East or if it was just a coincidence. . . . Right now
> it is kind of hard for me to determine what I think and feel
> about war and whether I think what we are doing is right or
> wrong. I think Richard Wilbur would never think that war is
> right.

Other students wrote about the beauty of the first snow while totally ignoring the dead soldiers beneath. In discussions, their classmates commented that they were missing the whole point of the poem. One of the offending students admitted, courageously, that given the world situation, she did not want to think about war. She did not think the narrator of the poem did either! These passionate and personal responses would probably not have emerged as a result of my questions. The students were using the sense they could make of the poem to make sense of their own relationships with and reactions to the world situation.

Even when journal entries seem less insightful, students are engaged in the process of exploration. Carole, a student who has struggled with English study guides in the past and who used to claim that she "didn't get it," used her journal entry on "First Snow in Alsace" to retell the plot of the poem. After a laborious page of retelling, she skipped a line and then wrote, "Maybe Richard Wilbur was the night guard. He sees the scene very well." Even though Carole's level of understanding is not as developed as other students', writing about the poem helped her to understand the surface level to the degree that she could make a guess about the author. She was pleased with her discovery. Reading poetry in school is no longer a totally frustrating activity for her.

Occasionally, students' observations in journals amaze me with their philosophical nature. Study guides or textbook questions could never require and would seldom elicit this level of perception. Shannan wrote a beautiful description of the sadness of "First Snow in Alsace" before she ended with this comment on the difference between reality and fiction:

> I think that because this is a real thing that someone saw, it's even more sad because we can picture it, but he was there. We can always escape, but the snow was his only escape.

At the beginning of the year, some of my students shared my concerns about the changes in classroom procedure. Some worried that, without study guides, they would have trouble studying for tests. Many wrote that they liked journals but that they learned more from study guides. They, too, thought of journals as peripheral to "real" learning. As the year progressed, their feelings changed, for the most part. On the first day of the second term, I asked them to reflect on their use of journals. Their responses simply confirmed my growing confidence that this method was the best I could use.

One student corroborated my initial premise when she wrote,

"Journals helped me learn more because in journals you ask your own questions." Although they worried earlier about knowing the "right" answers, their fears seemed to abate. Another student commented that "I really like journals. There you have the freedom to write anything that pops out of your head, and there's no real right or wrong answer. Whatever you write is right for you." Several students wrote that journals helped them discover "hidden points." Liz, a quiet and serious student, summed up the value of journal responses as exploration of literature: "The journals are effective because you could discuss the meaning of things with yourself." Isn't "discussing with yourself" what studying literature is really all about?

11 An Evolution in the English Class

Daniel D. Victor
Fairfax High School, Los Angeles, California

Anyone who has majored in English at college is familiar with those traditional literature courses that examine the lives and works of individual authors. Indeed, we English teachers are so cognizant of such semester-long examinations of writers like Milton and Shakespeare, that we often forget how many of our high school students have never thought at all about the connection between an author's life and his or her work—let alone about the ramifications of that relationship over the course of a career. Even those adolescents I have encountered who are deeply interested in literature have never given a great deal of consideration to the idea that authors mature and develop just like other people, that their early works may differ from their later efforts, and that much insight and understanding can be gained from identifying those changes. The remarkable discovery that an author's ideas and techniques may, in fact, evolve as the author's life progresses can lead even the most reluctant readers to a greater appreciation of the flesh-and-blood reality within those threatening tomes called "classics."

To achieve such benefits, I have my eleventh-grade advanced placement American literature class study not only the important works of writers such as Melville, Hawthorne, Dickinson, and Wright, but relevant biographies and critical essays as well. The major assignment itself is deceptively simple: After reading three to five major works by an author, as well as the related secondary sources, the students are to write a paper explaining to what extent and for what apparent reasons they believe an author's writings changed during the course of the writer's career.

Because such an approach is often surprisingly new to my students, I demonstrate what I want them to do by having the entire class follow my lead in exploring the career of Samuel Clemens. Clemens is a natural for such study. The autobiographical nature of so much of his fiction, the disturbing coincidences and reversals in so many of his narratives, and the critics' cries of outrage at posthumous tampering with his manuscripts engage young scholars in the subtleties of interpretation without alarming them unnecessarily about their participation in sophisticated literary criticism.

We approach Clemens's chronologically, linking the events in his life to the literature read in class. In addition to *Tom Sawyer, Huckleberry Finn, A Connecticut Yankee in King Arthur's Court,* and *The Mysterious Stranger,* students study autobiographical sketches like *Old Times on the Mississippi* and germane analytical pieces by prominent literary critics. Through weekly essays, the class evaluates the effects on Clemens's writing of such ironies as his less-than-affluent upbringing versus his parents' ill-fated hopes for wealth, his business failures in the face of his doggedness in reestablishing his finances, and his comic spirit against the ever-increasing bitterness prompted by the deaths of his son, his two daughters, and his wife.

If all has gone well, by the end of our study of Clemens (the remainder of the term is spent in preparation for the advanced placement language and composition exam), my students will be ready to undertake their own research and analysis on the author each has selected. Emboldened by such debates in class as those on the controversial ending of *Huckleberry Finn,* or the dubious merits of the generally accepted version of *The Mysterious Stranger*—which Clemens himself did not entirely compose—students are usually unafraid to criticize their own authors. For instance, one young lady, who empathized with Ferlinghetti's description of what she called "total powerlessness, the desperateness of having no control over one's life, and of not being able to distinguish between what is really *you* and what you have been made by our society" could nonetheless complain of what she regarded as his disturbingly antifeminist stance. "Ferlinghetti," she observed, "writes about liberation of the self, the fostering of the revolutionary and creative spirit, but nowhere is the inclusion of women in this visionary voice."

Without doubt, however, the most formidable aspects of the assignment are first identifying and then tracing the changes in the author's work. In some cases, students get into difficulty by choosing overly broad topics ("The American Dream," for example) or by overpersonalizing their responses ("How Thoreau Changed My Life"). Others may regard the truncated careers of authors like Stephen Crane or Lorraine Hansberry as not long enough for dramatic change to occur. But much more common is the student who just cannot identify any change at all (assuming some degree of modification has taken place—and invariably it has) and who therefore resorts to repeating static views of the same theme as it appears in different books.

Most students do discover significant issues, however, and the results are often impressive. One such effort highlighted Salinger's depiction of the "alienation suffered by sensitive and creative people"; another examined Lillian Hellman's view that "selfish action outweighs good moral values"; a third student identified what intrigued him in Poe: "In the murderer's fetish to kill, he frighteningly possesses many of the same characteristics often praised in sane men, such as patience and planning."

What's more, students who succeed in tracking the development of the themes they have discovered frequently gain insights that one does not generally find in high school classes. In his summary of the changes in the works of Dashiell Hammett, for example, one young man astutely chronicled the decline of the so-called "code of honor" for Hammett's heroes:

> Hammett's detectives describe an evolution of thought and character. Beginning with the Continental Op, one sees the nucleus of the code. . . . With Sam Spade the ethical detective reaches his pinnacle. The writing is taut and flows quickly, the ideas expressed are complex and compelling. Later . . . the code-hero becomes more than human, a being of pure code and no humanity, thereby eliminating the inherent conflict which makes code-heroes interesting. With Nick Charles we see the end of the code. The detective is burned out; he can't handle the strain of ethics anymore. In the grand finalé the great detective asks for a drink.

Needless to say, this type of assignment is most appropriate for students who possess deep interest in literature and literary analysis. But the ability to trace a theme is a useful skill for anyone learning to read critically, and since not all students need to be confronted with long reading lists or overly complex works, less-capable classes can also profit from highlighting simple contrasts in different works written by the same author. With guidance from insightful teachers and inspiration from challenging writers, high school students can be encouraged to create sophisticated literary analyses. By discovering the dynamic relationship between life and literature, these students can produce not only the kind of work more generally associated with college-level scholarship, but also the kind of reactions that signify a greater appreciation of fine literature.

12 Walk on a Rainbow Trail

Joel Kammer
Piner High School, Santa Rosa, California

This summer I chanced to spend some time in a California state park in the Sierra foothills, an area on the edge of the gold country. One evening my wife and I attended a "campfire," one of the historical or naturalist programs presented by the park staff each evening. We arrived a bit late, just as the seemingly obligatory campfire sing was beginning, and that evening's song was led by a member of the audience, a young father who seemed to be a park regular, well known to the ranger. He taught the audience a song about Eskimos hunting walrus, a song, much to the delight of the many children in the crowd, replete with gestures and facial expressions. The gestures in this song, however, included a series of grotesque grimaces, arms-folded "dance" steps, and somewhat subhuman grunts, not to mention a chorus featuring purportedly Inuit words which were actually gibberish.

As I watched this probably well-meaning man teach the delighted children this racist nonsense, with the apparent wholehearted approval of the ranger, it occurred to me that in an era of discrimination and racial hatred and violence, the first Americans may still have the most difficult path to equality. I certainly do not mean to minimize problems faced by other minority groups in the America of the nineties, but it is hard for me to imagine anyone getting away with such an insultingly stereotypical display aimed at any other group of people, at least on public property.

Similarly, it is difficult to imagine a major league sports franchise nicknamed the "Blackskins," "Brownskins," "Whiteskins," or "Yellowskins," but the Washington Redskins continue to be the darlings of football fans in our nation's capital; the grinning, buck-toothed, large-nosed caricature of the Cleveland Indian still adorns that team's caps; and "Chief Nokahoma" ("Knock-a-homer") used to patrol the area behind the left-field fence in Atlanta–Fulton County Stadium during Braves games, beating a tom-tom and shaking his feathered headdress to incite the crowd.

Despite the renewed activism of Native American groups in the new decade, despite the enormous popularity of the film *Dances with*

Wolves, despite many demonstrations, court cases, and educational efforts, a century after the massacre at Wounded Knee, precious little progress has been made toward the understanding of Indians by non-Indians. How can we, as teachers, help make our students aware of the past and present in Indian history and sensitize them to the heritages and cultures of Native Americans? Surely, one possible approach is through the study of literature, and I have found Tony Hillerman's Navajo mysteries an effective starting point for such exploration.

Since 1970, Hillerman, a former wire service reporter and university professor, has published ten mysteries featuring one or both of his fictional Navajo police officers, Joe Leaphorn and Jim Chee. Though he is not Indian himself, Hillerman is no plunderer of Navajo culture, nor does he simply employ Navajos as colorful background. Having grown up on an Oklahoma farm, he has developed an affinity for the "rural, poor, and isolated" Navajo culture. He "can talk to a Navajo [his] age and find [they] both grew up hauling water, depending on weather and livestock . . . not having the power to influence anything," having "a great deal in common" (Gaugenmaier 1989, 56). He tries to make his books as accurate as possible, and he is extremely careful about authentic detail. For example, in order to accurately depict the rarely performed Navajo ceremony called "yeibichai" for the beginning of his enormously popular *Talking God*, Hillerman delayed writing the final draft for several months when a Christmas Eve snowstorm closed roads and prevented him from attending the first yeibichai to which he had been invited (Crowder 1989, D6). Similarly, when Chee, a budding "yataali" (a singer, or healer, or "medicine man"), practiced a sand painting outdoors in chapter 18 of *Skinwalkers*, something a true Navajo shaman would only do inside a hogan, Hillerman felt obligated to add an author's note acknowledging the dramatic necessity for inaccuracy.

This respect for Navajo culture and attention to details is recognized by the Dinee (the Navajo people); in addition to several well-known awards he has received for his fiction, Hillerman has also been awarded the Navajo Tribe's Special Friend Award (1986), and his books are required reading in Navajo schools. St. Catherine's Indian School in Santa Fe, New Mexico, recently voted him its favorite author, and he is a frequent commencement speaker at Indian schools (Crowder 1989, D6). Some Navajo parents and teachers credit him with stirring up interest in the old ways among the tribe's young people (Gaugenmaier 1989, 58).

All ten novels reveal at least some of what Hillerman glimpsed about the Navajo. As he began writing the first of the series, *The Blessing Way*, in 1968, "[He] saw the possibilities of what you could do with the Navajo culture. [He] thought it was a good way to tell a story. A contrast between cultures and a way to put values in highlights" (Gaugenmaier 1989, 56). It is that contrast and the spotlight on values, along with the finely drawn characters and vivid settings, that make the books such effective teaching tools. From among the titles available last year, I chose his 1988 novel *Skinwalkers*, the seventh in the series and the first to bring together Leaphorn and Chee, to use with my students.

Before moving to some specific suggestions for teaching the novel, some brief background information seems appropriate. A "skin-walker," or "Navajo Wolf," is what many non-Indian cultures might refer to as a witch. Navajo mythology, including the role of witches within society, is one of the most frequently recurring aspects of tribal culture in Hillerman's fiction. He explores the idea of witchcraft directly or indirectly in virtually all the mysteries, but his concept is too involved and intricate for this discussion; in brief, however, it has to do with the Navajo view of life as being in harmony with one's surroundings. When that harmony is shattered, when one is out of harmony with nature or other people, a healer and a specific ceremony may be necessary to restore the balance. One who deliberately disrupts that harmony, by, say, committing an unprovoked act of violence is, by definition, a witch.

Whether this belief in witchcraft is actually part of traditional Navajo cosmology is open to debate; in *Skinwalkers*, Hillerman suggests that "belief in skinwalkers had no part in the Navajo culture, that the tribe had been infected with the notion while it had been held captive down at Fort Sumner" (72). There is no question, however, that the skinwalker concept influences the thinking of many Navajos. Dr. Tony Dajer of the Public Health Service writes that "even many younger, city-educated Navajos pay heed to the intricate, unseen forces of traditional belief," telling of a female hospital psychologist "trained at a well-known East Coast university" who "understood all about chromosomes and the laws of genetic probability." Yet, when she gave birth to a baby with Down's syndrome, she "remained convinced that her child was malformed because, while pregnant, she and her husband had seen a coyote . . . cross the highway ahead of them," which "disrupted her harmony," and she had not subsequently performed the "ritual ceremonies [required] to exorcise the omen" (Dajer 1989, 48).

This incident parallels the beginning of *Skinwalkers*, in which Chee's trailer is blasted by a shotgun-wielding woman who, having given birth to a malformed baby, has become convinced that Chee is the witch who has cursed her child, and that killing the skinwalker is the only way to restore the health of the baby. The belief in witches also separates college graduates Leaphorn (Arizona State), who despises such harmful superstitions, and Chee (University of New Mexico), who "like a nonfundamentalist Christian" believes "in the poetic metaphor of the Navajo story of human genesis" and "the lessons such imagery [were] intended to teach" (Dajer 1989, 73). Chee, the younger of the two detectives and, according to Hillerman, "the idealist . . . like the romantics that came along in the sixties" (Gaugenmaier 1989, 57), believes that "the origin story of the Navajos explained witchcraft clearly enough, and it was a logical part of the philosophy on which the Dinee had founded their culture. If there was good, and harmony, and beauty on the east side of reality, then there must be evil, chaos, and ugliness to the west" (Hillerman 1988, 73). Chee's musings and Navajo beliefs have obvious parallels in Anglo and East Asian thought and literature. Harmony with nature could be further explored in the writings of Thoreau or Dillard, and the interdependence of good and evil could be pursued in the works of authors as diverse as Camus, Shakespeare, Hesse, Forster, or Flannery O'Connor, to cite just a few obvious examples.

With my students, however, a mixture of low- to moderate-achieving high school seniors, I hoped to provide an opportunity for some integrated learning that encompassed geography, critical thinking, sociology, and human relations, choosing to emphasize the elements of plot (the tradition of mystery writing), theme (witchcraft), and setting (both the physical location of the Navajo reservation and the culture clash at the intersections of Navajo and Anglo societies). Therein, of course, lies much of Hillerman's tale, and there also, I believe, is the point from which to approach the novel as a teaching tool for my students; the suggestions I have are specific to *Skinwalkers*, but are applicable to any of Hillerman's books. Here, then, is one approach to teaching the novel.

Before distributing the books, I assess the knowledge or beliefs students already have about Indians, the "winning of the West," witchcraft, the Southwest, mysteries, etc. I use word association, having students write for a specific period of time (a stopwatched minute or two) everything they know about words or phrases such as "Navajos" or "Kit Carson" (a significant figure in Navajo history) or "witches"; I then call on each student, at least once, to give me an item of information, a belief, or a question he or she has written during the allotted time. I write the responses on the board in abbreviated form, putting checks next to items mentioned more than once. We air stereotypes, share knowledge, formulate questions, and stimulate interest, giving motivation for and direction to the reading they are about to do.

Next, I attempt to get beyond stereotypical thinking and give some factual foundation to the fiction they will read by providing information or, better, having students unearth information themselves. I assign short, specific projects, requiring a minimal amount of research, to be worked on concurrently with the reading and to be shared later with the class. Even if there are only minimal research facilities available at your school, there are some readily-available sources that can be most helpful: "The Long Walk of the Navajo," a chapter from Dee Brown's *Bury My Heart at Wounded Knee* (1970), is short, informative, and quite moving. A student or students could read it and summarize it to the class as historical background; it is equally powerful when read aloud and discussed in class. Back issues of *Arizona Highways,* some issues of *National Geographic,* encyclopedias, other books, films, interviews (with Native Americans, history teachers, etc.) are other possible sources of information that can help fill in the background and setting of the novel for students unfamiliar with Navajo or Indian history and culture. I ask students to compile information in written or graphic form. They may draw Navajo rug patterns, or traditional hogans, or turquoise jewelry and explain the significance of their artwork rather than deliver a factual summary report, if they so choose. I allow them to work individually or in groups.

An additional assignment I have used is to have students work with atlases or road maps to create their own maps of the reservation area in order to identify significant locations in the story, an activity which seems to help them keep the story's "facts" clearer in their minds. Another way to focus interest, either before or during reading, is to show the film *Koyaanisqatsi* (1983); the title is a Hopi word that can be translated as "life out of balance." The film brings together a vast array of striking visual images of America, both natural and man-made, from Indian rock paintings to Las Vegas casinos, backed by the relentless synthesizer music of Philip Glass and various Hopi chants. Either during or after the film, students can react to the images and the contrasts, discuss or write about how modern life is or is not balanced, reflect on the degree of harmony and balance in their own lives, or debate which aspects of life must be balanced to make life worthwhile. In so doing, they are preparing themselves to understand the dilemma of Jim Chee and modern Navajos (or any thinking persons, for that matter).

To begin the novel itself, I read the first chapter aloud, asking students to jot down questions that occur to them as I read. Students will certainly be puzzled about some things: Who is Mary Landon? What is so significant about the cat's entering Chee's trailer? What do the "yei" have to do with anything? Some questions will be answered before the chapter ends; some you will want to answer immediately to clarify words or ideas and avoid potential difficulties for students; some are integral to the mystery and should be saved for later, though, perhaps, discussed briefly at the time.

Variations to this assignment might be to have students write dialectical journal entries, questions for each other, or in some other way focus on connections, responses, questions, or doubts prompted by the first few chapters. I give students "detective's notebook" sheets as well. Mine are divided into sections labeled "Suspect's Information," "Victim's Information," "Physical Evidence," "Inferential/Testimonial Evidence," etc., providing students room to list clues and compile "facts" in an attempt to solve the crime along with the detectives. They record when, where, and how victims are dispatched, and who had motive, means, and opportunity to dispatch them. It helps them keep track of the numerous characters—many of whom have unusual or distinctive names—and to keep track of the investigations of the two detectives in a relatively coherent fashion. When focusing on the book as a mystery, I can then more easily demonstrate that Hillerman "played by the rules," planting all necessary correct information, along with the various red herrings, throughout the story.

I also give students chapter-by-chapter study questions and journal-style writing prompts aimed at keeping their attention focused on important aspects of the mystery as well as unique aspects of Navajo culture. Many prompts are designed to enable students to see connections between beliefs or customs, which at first seem odd or unique, and their own value and belief systems. Two good sources of such comparisons are Navajo beliefs regarding the mortality of skin-walkers and the superstitions of Navajos in general. According to believers, skinwalkers gain superhuman powers, the ability to "fly through the air, to run as fast as the wind can blow, to change themselves into dogs and wolves and maybe other animals" (*Skinwalkers*, 44). Witches shoot fragments of human bone through tubes, into the bodies of victims, creating a fatal "corpse sickness" which must be reversed by somehow shooting a bone bead or fragment into the witch—and bone beads are among the most important evidence in this mystery.

With a little prompting, even the most skeptical students, those most apt to dismiss all this as the superstitious nonsense of a "primitive" people, can easily recall the "facts" about European creatures of the night such as vampires, ghosts, werewolves, and zombies. Bone beads do not seem, then, any less credible than garlic necklaces, crucifixes as shields, or silver bullets. Students from other cultures and backgrounds may also provide variations on such dark myths that they are willing to share. For example, two years ago, a student of mine who had left Cambodia when he was quite young still vividly remembered a "witch" from his old village.

Another compelling aspect of Hillerman's writing is the vividness of the physical settings he creates. One reason for this quality is that much of his description is written firsthand: "Although I have been nosing around the Navajo Reservation and its borderlands for more than thirty years," he reveals in a *Writer* article (Hillerman 1986, 7), "I still revisit the landscape I am using before I start a new book— and often revisit it again while I am writing it. And then I write with a detailed, large scale map beside my word processor." His feel for the arid and stark landscape of the reservation and his ability to evoke the sensual details—the sounds and smells, as well as the sights of land, sky, and mountains—are fine examples of writing that puts readers "there," that "shows" rather than "tells" what a place is like. This feel for place comes through beautifully in Hillerman's prose. To cite just one example from *Skinwalkers*, there is his description of Chee racing a storm front into the remote backcountry of the reservation:

> Just past Piñon he had run into a quick and heavy flurry of rain—drops the size of peach stones kicking up spurts of dust as they struck the dirt road ahead of him. Then came a bombardment of popcorn snow which moved like a curtain across the road, reflecting his headlights like a rhinestone curtain. That lasted no more than a hundred yards. Then he was in dry air again. But rain loomed over him. It hung over the northeast slopes of Black Mesa like a wall—illuminated to light gray now and then by sheet lightning. The smell of it came through the pickup vents, mixed with the smell of dust. In Chee's desert-trained nostrils it was heady perfume—the smell of good

grazing, easy water, heavy crops of pinon nuts. The smell of
good times, the smell of Sky Father blessing Mother Earth. (238)

This is one of my favorite descriptions of weather, comparable in some
ways to Huck Finn's account of the storm lashing Jackson's Island as
he and Jim watched from the shelter of their cave; it is also useful as
a model for students. Using it, or another of the finely crafted
descriptions of place that dot Hillerman's work, have students write
their own descriptions of a favorite place—a refuge, a room, a beach,
a mall. The best papers can be read aloud, and the Navajo sense of
place, akin perhaps to the Spanish *querencia* and a concept important
to many cultures, will become clearer and more familiar to students.
This can also provoke some interesting and powerful discussions: How
do refugees from Southeast Asia or Central America feel about home,
new and old? How connected are native-born Americans to their
ancestors' homelands? Ask, for example, all students with Italian, or
Irish, or Mexican, or German heritage to raise their hands; what makes
them American but still Italian, for example? Are they more American
than more recently arrived immigrants? Are they less American than
Indians? Whose land is the United States, after all?

Depending on the makeup of your class and the willingness of
students to share their feelings and beliefs in an open but nonthreatening way, such writing and discussion can be the springboard to
greater understanding, not just of Navajo culture and its relationship
to the land and the predominant Anglo culture, but of the power and
potential inherent in the cultural diversity of the United States. And
it may also help students better understand what happens to individuals
and groups who are discriminated against or picked upon, who can
neither maintain their cultural integrity nor assimilate easily within
the larger society.

Works Cited

Brown, Dee. 1970. *Bury My Heart at Wounded Knee: An Indian History of the
American West.* New York: Holt, Rinehart & Winston.

Crowder, Joan. 1989. "Success of Navajo Stories Surprises Hillerman."
Santa Rosa *Press Democrat*, June 18, D6.

Dajer, Tony. 1989. "Medicine Man." *Discover* 10: 47+.

Gaugenmaier, Judith Tabor. 1989. "The Mysteries of Tony Hillerman."
American West 26: 46+.

Hillerman, Tony. 1986. "Building without Blueprints." *Writer* 19: 7–10.

———. 1988. *Skinwalkers*. New York: Harper & Row.

Koyaanisqatsi. 1983. Godfrey Reggio, Dir. Original music by Philip Glass. IRE.

13 Teaching Shakespeare in the Inner City

Elise Ann Earthman
San Francisco State University

Ten minutes into a new unit on *Macbeth*, the students had my number. Though it was midyear, they had just met me—I was a university professor who had appeared a few days before to teach them for one marking period. But when I launched into Shakespeare by talking about my own teenage love for the Bard, the question came lightning fast: "Mrs. Earthman, were you a *nerd?"*

I had to admit that I had been. At age fourteen, I discovered the *Collected Works* my mother had used in high school, and I was hooked. I wept over Juliet's fate, memorized her lines, acted them out in front of a mirror— then did the same for Ophelia and Lady Macbeth. Shakespeare reached through time and distance to seize my nerdy heart, and I have loved him ever since.

But my seniors, inner-city minority students, did not share this affection. When I asked them to freewrite on their past encounters with Shakespeare, I got what I expected, for they were the same comments I hear from my university students: "It's boring. It's jibber-jabber. It's about olden times. It's not about life today." How could I begin to open up the process of response to these students? Is it possible to help street-sophisticated, worldly-wise modern young people, whether high school or lower-division college students, to connect with Shakespeare, or must he remain the secret passion of teenage geeks who will one day become English teachers?

I train teachers for both the high school and college levels, and I was brought to Mission High School by a new California program that keeps its university-level education people in touch with the public schools. Mission presents students, teachers, and administrators alike with the challenges typical of an inner-city school. The student population is diverse in every way, from ethnic and racial backgrounds, to motivation and ability with English as a native or second language. Classes are large and noisy. Students come and go, their attendance often affected by individual and family problems.

Macbeth was my choice. Bolstered by the successful techniques I had used with my college students, I decided to try Shakespeare with these high school seniors, and in doing so, to confront the same kinds of challenges that my secondary education students do when they go out to practice-teach in urban California.

Recent curriculum decisions in California and other states bring together two seemingly divergent trains of thought: the notion of core works that all students should read and the reader-response school of literary theory. Students are to read "core literary works . . . [that] offer all students a common cultural background from which they can learn about their humanity, their values, and their society" (English Language Arts Curriculum Framework and Criteria Committee 1987, 7), and this program will be made available to *all* students, no matter what their reading level or ability with the English language may be. At the same time, the new curriculum emphasizes that the approach to literature will be meaning-centered, that life experience and literature should be integrated, and that diversity of experience and opinion will be respected.

If we think about fulfilling these two requirements at the same time, while reflecting on what we know about the reading process, we can develop a chicken-or-egg kind of headache. Although we may argue long and loud about what constitutes a "common culture," we do want students to acquire knowledge from *Macbeth* and many other works, because we know the importance of background knowledge acquired in reading—without it, our students will be handicapped as they try to reach higher levels of education and literacy. And this "information" must not be taught outside the context of the literature. At the same time, we want students to enjoy Shakespeare, to truly connect with *Macbeth*—isn't this what we dream of, the reason we became English teachers?

To engage in the kind of transaction that reader-response theorists have described in different ways, students need a great deal of knowledge and experience that they may not have, and often, as Rosenblatt (1976) points out, the background information they do have can be "irrelevant and distracting." So how do we bring together a difficult text and nontraditional readers, helping them along the way to write the "cogent, clear, and concise prose connected to the literary work," also required by the *Model Curriculum Standards* (California State Board of Education 1985, E-1)? What happens when the Upstart Crow meets the Mission Bears, when the world of Macbeth and Lady Macbeth collides with the world of Priscilla Wong or Richie Martinez?

Reader-response theorists such as Rosenblatt, Fish, and Iser have taught us a great deal about how the literary transaction takes place. But these scholars assume very willing and active readers who bring to the text a good deal of knowledge of literature and experience with life. Rosenblatt (1978) states that "the selection and organization of [a reader's] responses to some degree hinge on the assumptions, expectations, or sense of possible structures that he brings out of the stream of his life" (11). But because my students were convinced that Shakespeare offered them nothing, the sense of the possible that they brought out of the stream of *their* lives seemed likely to bring the literary process to a halt before it even began.

I work to engage my students, because all of reader response hinges on this idea—unless a reader is engaged, the transaction will not take place; there will be no meaningful response. I think about the notion of engagement on two or three different levels—first, the students need to engage with me as a teacher, to become partners in the process of learning; second, students need to be engaged with the literature itself, with the stories, the characters; and finally, students need to engage with the ideas and themes found in the literature and to feel that these themes are relevant to their lives.

As teachers, we all know ways of engaging students. For me, the most important tool is the journal. We have heard over and over how valuable journals are in improving students' writing; theorists have advocated their use, and researchers have documented their positive effects. But I have an ulterior motive when I use journals—they are my main vehicle for establishing a relationship with my students, one through which I can represent myself as someone who welcomes their insights and takes them seriously. Students engage with me personally through journals, and this engagement creates a better atmosphere in the classroom, one with more interaction and fewer management problems. I asked my students at Mission to write a number of journals at the beginning of the quarter, so I could let them know I was interested in them as individuals and in what they had to say. For many of them, this was a new experience. We continued to do informal writing-to-learn, in and out of class, on almost a daily basis. Generally, I tend to start out with more personal topics and then move to more literature-based topics, though ones that still call for students' opinions and input.

Next, I helped my high school seniors connect with the literature itself. First, I organized the unit with a theme relevant to late adolescence—the idea of making choices and living with those choices—

and selected two other, much shorter and easier works that supported that theme. Before reading *Macbeth,* the students read a Thomas Hardy short story, "To Please His Wife," about a woman named Joanna who lies and schemes to get a man she does not love, just because her best friend really loves him. The choices Joanna makes clearly arise out of her greed and ambition, and the consequences are disastrous for both her and her relationships.

After we finished *Macbeth,* students read John Collier's "The Chaser," about a young man who, out of desire and lust, makes a choice he will clearly regret at some point in the future. In addition, students were required to read a novel outside of class, chosen from a list of books featuring characters who made difficult choices and who could easily be compared or contrasted with Macbeth. These books included everything from "classic" works such as *Wuthering Heights* and *Great Expectations,* to popular adult novels such as David Brin's *The Postman,* to adolescent novels such as *The Killing of Mr. Griffin* and *The Chocolate War.*

Beyond using the Hardy story as a prelude to *Macbeth,* we set the stage in other ways as well. Students went to the library to do their own research on Shakespeare's life, daily life in Elizabethan times, and the history of the play, the results of which they shared in class. Students were interested in one another's presentations, especially when they found out, for example, that Shakespeare was hinted to be (in their words) a "lady killer." We did other exercises that gave the play a context and made the situation familiar to them. In one, students further explored the idea of fate—they were given a ditto that contained horoscopes for the rest of their lives. Students were to find their horoscope and write about whether they would accept this fate; in each case, the fate was something quite desirable, but one that came at a great cost. On another day, they read the *Macbeth* story retold in a modern high school setting and enjoyed arguing about the situation and who was at fault.

Our typical approach to Shakespeare, a protracted struggle through 400-year-old words, with a short-answer/multiple-choice test at its end, is frustrating for students and teachers alike. In this class, we took an actor's perspective on *Macbeth.* I told them how actors prepare for roles and how actors and directors make interpretive choices. We focused on the ideas of motivation, point of choice in a scene, and particularly *subtext*—here's what the character is saying on the surface, but what does he *really* mean underneath? We used acting exercises to illustrate the idea of subtext. We did directed readings of key scenes throughout the play—students performed scenes with minimal props and costuming, and we tried to maintain a sense of actors in preparation.

Instead of viewing one video of *Macbeth* at the end of the unit, we compared two versions of key scenes throughout—the BBC version, essentially a filmed stage play, and Roman Polanski's exciting movie version. Immediately after we had discussed a key scene and had students perform it, we watched two versions of the same scene on video. Students evaluated the two versions—for example, after viewing several scenes involving Lady Macbeth, they pondered the two characterizations, including Polanski's significant cuts, and wrote in groups about which they preferred. (Interestingly, these "nontraditional" students proved themselves traditionalists when it came to Shakespeare—they overwhelmingly preferred the BBC Lady Macbeth.) Though our focus and terminology may have been unusual, we still talked throughout about interpretation, about choices writers and characters make, and we approached many traditional literary concepts through a side door, so to speak.

Using an acting perspective helped me to incorporate an important premise from reader-response theory, one which has been validated through research: when we read literature, it is crucial that we hold ourselves open to possibilities and that we do not, in Rosenblatt's terms, "fix" on an interpretation too quickly. A recent study (Earthman 1989) showed that this is a problem for student readers—they want to get to an "answer" as soon as possible, and then they doggedly stick with that answer, no matter what. So considering different acting choices, in both the student run-throughs and the video versions, helped students think in terms of possibilities.

Other class activities focused on possibilities as well; at one point, I gave students a handout of quotations from critics who go head-to-head on various issues of interpretation of *Macbeth*. The students worked in pairs to decide which opinion they agreed with and to find evidence from the text to support their position. We discussed their positions in class, and they finally wrote one of their unit essays on the old argument about whether Macbeth acted from free will or was under the spell of the witches and Lady Macbeth. But in this case, students were not force-fed preconstructed positions which they were expected to repeat at the appropriate time; they built their essays from support they had developed on their own. They were also free to reject either of the "professional" opinions and come up with an alternative.

In addition, I asked students to write a short paper in which they speculated on the identity of the Third Murderer, stressing that there was no right answer to this question, only possibilities that were convincingly or not-so-convincingly argued. I also used students' journal writings to open up possibilities; after writing on all the ways in which "things are not what they seem" in the first part of the play, students received a handout of "Ideas from Your Journals" that enumerated all the possibilities they had come up with. One key to teaching literature of any kind, but particularly *great* literature to nontraditional students, is to disabuse them of the notion that they do not have anything to say about it, that it has all been said before, and that their job is to sit back and be passive receptacles while we zip open their heads and pour in the wisdom of the ages. It is hard work to do this, but by asking students for their opinions and welcoming their input, we can begin to change this attitude.

My final concern was getting the students engaged with the ideas and themes of the play, and again, I did this in a number of ways. Throughout the six weeks, we returned to the idea of choices and consequences, and we took up this theme in the questions for the essay which the students wrote at the end of the unit. The topics for this essay, fairly open-ended looks at character and theme, allowed students to choose which of the unit's four works to focus on and invited them to add insights gained from their own experience. Students also did nonwritten projects on *Macbeth* which were highly successful—we watched students acting out scenes they had rewritten into modern English, marveled over beautiful period costumes that several students had sewn, and listened to tapes of music they had made to accompany the play. In addition, part of the report the students did on their independent reading required an explicit connection to *Macbeth*—students wrote a letter to Macbeth from a character they selected, giving Macbeth advice. A number of these—from Pip, Clyde Griffiths, Heathcliff—were delightful.

Students responded enthusiastically to this unit; they did excellent work and they enjoyed it. Their comments are revealing:

> I think *Macbeth* is very good. Once I got past the language, I really liked the story. It was something I could relate to.

> I think *Macbeth* is wonderful. There was mystery in the play. After every act, I wanted to keep reading because it was really interesting.

> Reading literature can be exciting!

Interestingly, as reluctant as the students were at first to get up and act in the play—and I had to use every ounce of my persuasive powers to get them up there—their responses to the activity were overwhelmingly positive. One student wrote in his journal:

> *Macbeth* is not what I expected it to be. I thought it was going to take forever to read it. I also thought it would be about Romans. All the past English teachers have said nothing but, "If you think this is hard, just wait until you read *Macbeth*." Then when we had to read it, I was down in the mouth and disappointed. I told myself I had to overcome this sorrow. So I acted and made the audience laugh and enjoyed it also. *Macbeth* was more fun than what I thought it would be.

We can and should teach great literary works for a number of reasons, but I think my best one, the reason that made me become an English teacher, is the most personal—I love these works and I want students to love them too, to get the pleasure and enrichment that I have out of a play like *Macbeth*. They can do so, but their response is not immediate—we must create the conditions that will help them connect with literature so remote from them in time and place. However, the results can be exciting for both students and teacher, as my encounter with the Mission students has shown.

Works Cited

California State Board of Education. 1985. *Model Curriculum Standards: Grades Nine Through Twelve.* Sacramento: California State Department of Education.

Earthman, Elise Ann. 1989. "The Lonely, Quiet Concert: Readers Creating Meaning from Literary Texts." Ph.D. diss. Stanford University. *DAI* 50/06A, p. 1583.

English-Language Arts Curriculum Framework and Criteria Committee. 1987. *English Language Arts Framework.* Sacramento: California State Department of Education.

Rosenblatt, Louise M. 1976. *Literature as Exploration.* 3rd ed. New York: Modern Language Association.

———. 1978. *The Reader, The Text, The Poem: The Transactional Theory of the Literary Work.* Carbondale: Southern Illinois University Press.

14 Offering Literature with Respectful Deception

Carol Meinhardt
Springfield High School, Springfield, Pennsylvania

Learning is at its best when it's deadly serious and very playful at the same time.

—Sara Lawrence Lightfoot

I am not going to try to deceive you the way I tricked my students. You would see right through my machinations. I will confess, then, at the start: several years ago, I devised a backhanded way to offer Shakespeare's *Romeo and Juliet* to tenth graders, one that ultimately made the Bard's plot and words fairly relevant and unintimidating. More than that, however, in the process of my students' participation in their own deception, they really came alive in the classroom and never stopped being present for the rest of the school year. For me, the experience confirmed some pedagogical views I had been pondering, and consequently, ever since, I have had greater freedom in my teaching. I am excited about sharing with you what happened.

These students, labeled college bound, were essentially of average ability. With them, as with students in all my other classes, I was struggling with my eternal teaching question: How do I attend to the prescribed course of study for English, but also give my students vital reading material for which we all might have a fresh response? One day, with that perplexing question on my mind, I found myself staring in the direction of my bookshelves. There, stacked neatly, was a copy of *Romeo and Juliet,* a work that had allowed me, when teaching it in depth, to soar to great heights. Now it was just a book on the shelf, a title in the school curriculum, a paperback whose reputation had preceded it so that students were prepared to get no surprises when they were mandated to read it. At that moment, I had reached what you and I call the point of no return—a climax. I believed I had two options left for my survival: (1) rebel and personally finance a set of lesser-known but captivating works guaranteed to be less predictable (I had just finished reading Oliver LaFarge's haunting Indian love story, *Laughing Boy,* and thought it would work well); or (2) compromise and stick with the curriculum, but drastically alter my previous way of approaching fiction in a fairly linear manner.

In response to my dilemma, I conjured up "The Great Play Script Deception." One night, chuckling as I reinvented and twisted my source, I wrote seven ideas for short, modern play scenes. The next day, I offered a typed copy to each student (figure 1). The scenes add up loosely, in a contemporary fashion, to the story of Romeo and Juliet. I steered my students in a different direction. "Stick with me," I said. "It looks as though I pulled this stuff out of the blue, but there's a method to this madness—and a goal." Over a two-week period, I did not notice one student who cared what the goal was, other than his or her own pleasure in the involvement of the project. The students simply enjoyed the true-to-life situations and responded to them. In addition, no one noted the similarity between Shakespeare's story line and the sum of these scenes, and I encouraged that blindness. Then, one Monday, while the students laughed over episodes of the television show "Saturday Night Live," which I had seen, I had to force myself not to stamp my feet, throw my arms into the air, and yell, "Didn't you *get* Whoopi Goldberg's parody of the balcony scene? Don't you *know* you're doing the same thing?"

For two weeks, without the students having the same end in mind as I had, and while we were involved in other activities (e.g., reading and writing about the subject of love—since I wanted to prepare for Valentine's Day, when I would introduce *Romeo and Juliet*), my students worked harmoniously together. They organized, divided labor, and produced on a regular schedule. Finally, the groups were so excited about delivering their work that they moved up the performance dates and contacted the school's audiovisual department to tape the scenes. Because only a few came to me with questions about how to set up a play on paper, I did not feel obligated to teach the form. However, I did tell them not to worry about correctness but certainly to produce readable copy for everyone. I noticed a few pulling paperbacks of plays from the bookcase and paging through them briefly. It occurred to me during this time that I had observed this kind of dynamic before in the classroom. In my teaching, whenever I had allowed my students to move to the forefront, they had assumed an easy independence, and I naturally fell into the background. A controlling, dramatic teacher has difficulty accommodating this change, but I was truly enjoying the diminished responsibility.

The performances lasted three days instead of the scheduled two, but the level of interest never waned. Every group used highlighted

Ideas for Short, Modern Play Scenes

Directions: Re-create one of the scenes below by embellishing on the sketchy nature of my offering. Present your skit in front of the class. Write scripts, use them or memorize the lines, assemble minimal props and costumes, and deliver effectively. Consider using backdrops and background music. Each person in the group will receive the same grade for the overall effect of the performance. I would expect the skits to run at least ten minutes.

Situation #1: Street scene, 4 youths

Two youths (preppy types) are standing and goofing around when two other youths (druggie types) come along. The parents of both groups have warned their children to stay away from the other youths since there have been previous physical battles between them, and even police involvement. Nonetheless, neither side can completely contain itself, and finally, a conflict ensues.

Situation #2: Big party, 2 youths

A boy and a girl, both with the intention of catching the eye of a particular romantic interest at the party, suddenly and unexpectedly become attracted to one another. The meeting of these strangers is one of those special moments of recognition, and neither of the two can attend to anyone or anything but the other.

Situation #3: Open field, 4 youths

Three boys are hanging out together in an open field. Suddenly, an outsider appears to keep up a longstanding argument with one of the three and challenges him to a knife fight. This pursued boy avoids the physical challenge because he is aware of the aggressor's history of mental illness and erratic behavior. Consequently, the pursued boy takes quite a bit of abuse until one of his friends, unaware of why his buddy is so passive, decides to stand up for him. This friend ends up getting killed, but in the course of events, he appears the most energetic, appealing, and courageous of all.

Situation #4: Secret meeting place, boy and girl

Boy and girl of different races (or religions or nationalities) fall in love with one another. They know that their parents would be strongly opposed to the relationship because each family has judged members of the other group as unsuitable for mixing with them and somehow threatening. The boy and girl are headstrong and passionately involved and, therefore, push on with their arrangements for seeing one another regularly.

Situation #5: Home scene, girl and her parents

This girl, unbeknown to her parents, has become pregnant with the child of a boy she loves and plans to marry. She is waiting for the boy to get a job and begin earning money to support her and the child before she breaks the news. Meanwhile, the girl's parents, unbeknown to her, have decided to give her the money for a college education, money they earlier said she would have to earn. They want her to follow up on one of the college acceptances she has had to turn down. The girl tries to stall for time; the parents want her to make plans immediately so as not to miss an opportunity.

continued on next page

Figure 1. "The Great Play Script Deception."

Figure 1 continued

Situation #6: Home scene, boy and his friend's parents
   A fifteen-year-old boy and the parents of his best friend are standing in the parents' living room. The boy is trying to explain his good intentions that ultimately brought about his best friend's death, one the parents are not yet aware of.

Situation #7: Isolated spot, boy and girl
   A handsome boy and beautiful girl have fallen deeply in love and have made private vows to remain mates until death. The two are very different; she is popular, athletic, and successful in school; he is withdrawn, rather unproductive, and unsuccessful in academic matters. One day the girl comes upon the body of her boyfriend, who has committed suicide after a long depression over his low motivation. The knife he used for the suicide is laying at his side. The girl, who truly believes the boy is her soul mate for eternity, must choose between going on without him or anyone else for the rest of her life or killing herself as the boy has done.

---

scripts or lines on cards, but no one slavishly read from these papers. In the first scene, where the gangs fight, an all-male group brashly confronted each other, made coarse remarks (as in the original), and ended up in a free-for-all. An all-female group, doing the same scene, played it much more subtly and insidiously. They used only words, never fists, to send home the attack. I observed that the latter presentation kept the audience much more involved, though less amused.

Two creative, shy boys really shocked me by prophetically introducing into Situation #2 (the party) characters I had not mentioned in my suggestion: a Benvolio-type companion and a Rosaline-type romantic interest who gets jilted. At first, I thought they had uncovered my trick, but eventually I realized that they simply wanted more characters in order to pull off a tour de force. Eddie, playing the romancer, and Eric, playing the male companion (and, subsequently, both female parts), started out at the long conference table along the wall. They had decorated it with blinking, colored patio lights and had carelessly arranged Eddie's empty liquor bottle collection on top. Soon, the male friend slipped away, to return as a plain, rather aggressive girl. Eddie, with all the awkwardness and insensitivity youth can muster up, humorously rebuffed this acquaintance, who finally ran away in tears. We waited several minutes for Eric to return as a voluptuous female (quite unlike my image of the one who taught the torches to burn bright). Her eyes met with Eddie's, his advances were no less awkward than his earlier rejections, and they came together in an embrace. (I kept reminding myself to keep professional control and not laugh louder than the others.) In the postperformance evaluations, someone had written about Eddie and Eric's performance: "This play was definitely the funniest. Miss Meinhardt certainly seemed to think so, too."

Probably the most successful scene was the last, where the ambitious, successful girl becomes involved with the melancholic, self-destructive young man. The boy and girl who played the scene typecast themselves, he being hyperactive and basically nonachieving in school, she highly responsible and rewarded for her efforts. Although the students loved seeing their peers admit to and exaggerate their real qualities, they also seemed to be attending to the seriousness of the fictional situation. On one of the postperformance evaluations, a student noted, "My thoughts were on baseball cards until Scene 7 with Jessica and Mike. It had much humor in it as well as a serious, romantic side." In the same way, in an earlier scene, where the girl tries to tell her parents about her romantic relationship with a boy and her consequent pregnancy, the students only mildly laughed at the planned humor in the piece, but gave the group their full attention throughout, as though they were seeing a stage drama. A classmate wrote, "There were some laughs, but the more serious theme came through. You would never have known they only had two weeks to get this performance together."

By Valentine's Day, the groups had finished, and I was able to move in with the next stage of my plan, a dry one-page summary of *Romeo and Juliet*. Soon, students who decided to read started lighting up and shouting out, "Hey, this is me" and "Here's our scene" and "This is exactly what we just did." Then the interest became contagious, but no one accused me of deception or acted cheated. In fact, they paid no attention to me or to Shakespeare, but sat proudly for the next ten minutes rehashing their performances and praising themselves for coming so close to an already-set scene. I finished the period by reading Jesse Stuart's beautiful short story, "Love," about a bullsnake which risks its life to be close to its dead mate and a young boy's understanding of the depth of that affection. I was quite pleased with the way the pieces of that lesson fit together, but in retrospect, I realize most of Stuart's lovely images were lost to my students' absorption in their own, rough material.

The next day, we began reading Shakespeare together, and continued until we finished. I noticed many striking differences between this sharing activity and the previous ones, where I had offered the play for my students' enlightenment, rather than to already-enlightened people for their enjoyment. Here are some of the ways these students conducted themselves that most impressed me:

1. Most students volunteered to read.

2. At least half voluntarily stood to read.

3. Group members competed to read their parallel scene in Shakespeare.

4. Students asked questions about murky textual matters.

5. Some students wanted to investigate language and did so.

6. A few students, the ones who seemed to have the most involvement in the play, offered criticism along the way by pointing out inconsistencies and weak sections, as well as virtues.

7. Students answered other students' questions and eventually stopped looking to me for all the answers.

8. Most students looked interested, most of the time.

9. We finished the play on a high note, with people still chatting and debating across the rows.

10. The students dealt with the play as if it were written by a fallible human being, rather than a god whose words they must learn to decipher and then revere.

I have not used "The Great Play Script Deception" since that time, several years ago. I like it enough to want to try it again in some way, but now the trick won't be so easy to perpetrate. In the pure workshop environment I now establish in my classroom, my students are accustomed to choosing the titles they will read as well as the forms and topics for their writing. If I presented a modernized version of *Macbeth*, for instance, they might easily say, "Hey, that sounds like *Macbeth*; we heard the other reading group talking about it." And as I hemmed and hawed, they might continue, "Let's take that sheet as a model. We'll write our own scenes, maybe after we read the play." And I would definitely say, "Sure, do it," and not be surprised at all if they then went on to create an entire show.

Let me encourage you to try your version of "The Deception" at least once. Many of you know familiar, classic plays so well that you could easily summarize, divide, and update the story lines and have fun in the process. Some of you would also enjoy putting some fire under students' complacent responses to the classroom and to literature. But I think "The Deception" is more valuable than just being another creative way to draw students into our often introspective, sometimes esoteric discipline. More important, this activity and others like it teach us a simple truth about our students and the way we approach them, a truth we cannot afford to forget: all that we want our students to learn, they already carry within themselves. If we provide comfortable, purposeful environments where they can exercise a high degree of autonomy, they will know how to work together to organize and plan and produce. They will understand the need for certain forms, for correctness, clarity, and creativity. When we come to recognize their inherent strengths and praise them, our students will sit down feeling like partners with Shakespeare and Stuart, for example. They will know they are up to the task of responding to art and literature because they will have a sense of their own power as practitioners of the same craft.

15 The Collaborative Term Paper

JoAnna Stephens Mink
Mankato State University

Within the past few years, many composition researchers have explored the relationship between cognitive learning styles and writing. Consequently, in several books and articles we find suggestions, informed by the findings of psychologists and cognition theorists, of ways to integrate collaborative learning techniques into writing courses, particularly in technical writing, business writing, and most recently, in freshman composition courses. In her article "Interactive Learning in the Composition Classroom," Caryl Sills (1988) says that "cooperative learning is . . . a deliberate attempt to take advantage of differing perspectives through the interaction of individuals and their ideas in a reciprocal or alternating action (21). Collaborative learning is dependent upon positive interaction among group members as they work toward a common goal: "Students put into groups are only students grouped and are not collaborators, unless a task that demands consensual learning unifies the group activity" (Wiener 1986, 55).

I'll not elaborate more fully here on the value of collaborative learning. Suffice it to say that more and more instructors in more and more departments are making use of the research on group learning. The common concern is to plan activities that will meet the needs of students with differing learning styles, all of whom happen to be together in the same classroom. The assignment described below illustrates a way of integrating collaborative learning with the writing of a research project. I use this assignment in my sophomore-level introduction to drama course at Mankato State University.[1] Typically, not all of the thirty-five students enrolled in this course have met their freshman composition requirements, and most are neither English nor theatre majors.

The purpose of each paper, written by a group of four students, is to discuss a play from our reading list in terms of how the students would produce that play; in other words, they are to plan the transfer of the play script to the stage. Prior to this assignment, each of the students had written several reader-response journal entries about various plays, plus a paper interpreting a specific aspect of a play—typical undergraduate fare. The students had also had opportunities to work with other class members in pairs and in small groups. Consequently—and this is an important point—they had had some interaction with at least a few other class members before deciding upon their groups for this project. Also, at the very beginning of the course, while going over the syllabus, I spent quite some time describing this particular project and occasionally reminded them of it. I wanted them to choose group members whom they thought were congenial as well as capable students (though I never offered any guidance on this point). Although a few students had participated in group projects for other courses, none had written a collaborative paper on a literary text before participating in this assignment. Therefore, my instructions were fairly specific, while allowing for individual flexibility (figure 1). The assignment met these important criteria for effective group learning:

1. The duration was long enough (4 weeks) for effective group cohesion to occur.
2. There was time for leadership to emerge and for negotiation of authority.
3. The assignment involved types of tasks (the instructions indicated a possible breakdown of labor) including research, writing, typing, artwork.
4. Group members could build upon individual expertise.
5. There was opportunity for student self-evaluation as well as evaluation of group members. I used their individual evaluations in determining the grades. Individually—and outside of class—they filled out a confidential evaluation form on participation by all members of the group. I used their comments and my own observations in assigning the individual portion of the research paper grade.

Here is just a brief description of the innovative approaches which two student groups took in staging *The Misanthrope* by Molière. As one can see, students had to first read carefully and understand the play before they could make production decisions.

One group decided to place its play, retitled "Rebel Against Conformity," in a typical American drive-in of the 1950s because, group members said, "while the French had the salon, the fifties had their own institution of social gathering, the typical drive-in." Char-

---

Instructions

The purpose of the group assignment is to plan how to produce a play, moving from the script to the stage interpretation. The role the group assumes is mostly that of the director, as it creates the artistic and dramatic dimensions of the play as scripted by the playwright.

The group members are to consider the following elements of the production:

Stage Set: Whether the set description is sparse or very full, the group needs to decide how closely to adhere and to consider what would motivate major change. The group needs to select the type of stage, the time period, the elaborateness of the design, and to consider how important the set is to the action of the play. The presentation could include written descriptions and drawings or renderings.

Costumes: Costumes should serve to aid in understanding and interpreting the play, and they should be designed in conjunction with decisions about the set. Of course, the costumes must coordinate with the time period selected. A bare set might be offset by elaborate costumes. Both written description and drawings would be appropriate. Color and fabric should be specified.

Actors: The group may design physical descriptions of those who are to play the roles, or they might select actors from those currently appearing on stage, television, and screen. Selections need to match the way the character is developed in the play. Deviations from what the script calls for need to be rationalized.

Lighting and Sound: Consider special requirements for these technical aspects, and spell them out in some detail. Decide what music, if any, will be used.

The paper may be prepared by dividing up the work. All major decisions should be made by consensus. The teacher will be available for consultation but will not make individual assignments. Each project will be given a single grade. Individual grades may be influenced by the report of the other students in a confidential evaluation, and also by the teacher's observations.

Figure 1. Instructions for the collaborative term paper.

acters included Alceste, the rebel, wearing a black leather jacket over a white t-shirt, black denim jeans, and black loafers (à la James Dean), and Celimene, the new girl in town, in a light pink and puffy skirt. Thus, the set and the costumes were of the fifties era, although the actors spoke in couplets, as in Molière's play. Their rationale was to demonstrate that the hypocrisy and shallowness of sixteenth-century French society was still alive in 1950s America. Continuing to use couplets, they believed, would reinforce this similarity.

Another group placed *The Misanthrope* in a typical sorority house on a typical college campus. The red and blue letters of the sorority were emblazoned on white articles of clothing, symbolizing the social hypocrisy on American college campuses. Actors would wear typical college student clothing and the characters' names were modernized, demonstrating that hypocrisy and character types continue to exist. Alex/Alceste, a senior art major, is a pessimistic rebel out to reform society. Phil/Philinte majors in public relations and is student body president. In contrast to Alex's dark complexion, Phil has blond hair and blue eyes, and speaks in a warm, friendly voice. Sally/Celimene, a junior in speech communication, is a cheerleader and sorority president. She wears heavy makeup, and in the salon scene, reclines on the couch and does her nails. Oron/Oronte is a junior music major, enrolled in "Introduction to Contemporary Composing," so instead of reading a sonnet, he shares with Alex the lyrics of a rock song.

There were a few problems with this assignment, which may not apply to each institutional setting, but which can be easily overcome. My class met three times a week, and while I arranged class time for group meetings and workshops, several students indicated they had difficulty getting together outside of class because of other commitments. What I will emphasize in the future is that all group members do not have to meet every time the group meets; in fact, with allocation of tasks within the group, members could do much of the work independently and assimilate it during their class workshop time. Another problem was that, in a couple of groups, one or two members shirked their fair share of the work. I had warned them that this kind of thing can easily happen in almost any group project. Since I teach at the college level and assume that students can behave as adults, I basically told each group that they had to work this situation out themselves but that they would have a chance to tell me about any problems (and a couple of students did receive F's for their individual grade). All in all, these problems were rare and, on the whole, did not detract from the overall success of the assignment.

The comments from the evaluation questionnaire that the students completed were overwhelmingly positive. Following are a few representative comments:

> It [the assignment] was a difficult thing to do, but it was a growing experience.

> . . . I think students need more of these types of projects. You learn more than just about drama.

It was something worth doing. Working with others gets you motivated to do a good job; the others won't let you get by without doing your share of work.

[You] can't procrastinate. Must do your work on time or 3 people get pulled down with you.

I think it was interesting to find pictures of what the stage and costumes were like in the 1700s.

Over and over again, students commented that the most enjoyable aspect of this assignment was getting to know other students in the class and exchanging ideas with their peers. I believe this assignment was successful for the students because:

1. It gives students the opportunity to work with other students informally, to share ideas, and to learn from each other.
2. It provides an alternative to the typical research paper, which is prepared and written in isolation.
3. Students learn to share responsibility and to work together toward a common goal.
4. The assignment encourages students to look beyond the words written on the paper as they experience elements of drama not normally covered in a survey literature course.

In addition, the assignment was fun and interesting for me because it provided me with an opportunity to work with students in their small groups, something usually impossible in classes of thirty-five students, and because their papers—much more creative than I had anticipated—were interesting to read. An added bonus (which I honestly had not anticipated) was that instead of reading thirty-five research papers representing varying degrees of quality, I read nine stimulating plans for production. I plan to use this assignment again, whenever possible.

Note

1. The germ for this assignment came from Fred Rubick, a theatre faculty member at Elon College in North Carolina, at a 1990 writing-across-the-curriculum conference sponsored by the University of North Carolina at Charlotte. Rubick's point was that students must demonstrate their knowledge by application to a specific event or performance.

Works Cited

Lawrence, Gordon. 1982. *People Types and Tiger Stripes: A Practical Guide to Learning Styles.* Gainesville, FL: Center for Applications of Psychological Types, Inc.

Sills, Caryl Klein. 1988. "Interactive Learning in the Composition Classroom." In *Focus on Collaborative Learning,* edited by Jeff Golub and the Committee on Classroom Practices, 21–34. Urbana: NCTE.

Wiener, Harvey S. 1986. "Collaborative Learning in the Classroom: A Guide to Evaluation." *College English* 48: 52–61.

16 Connecting with the Classics

Barbara Jones Brough
Anderson High School, Cincinnati, Ohio

Most of our students will get along without knowing the terms *caesura* or *kenning*. And they can probably survive without undertaking an in-depth analysis of the dynamics of metaphysical poetry. But they will not be able to get through life without realizing that no person is an island or that the past and the present are not all that different. Knowing the wisdom and vision of the literary sages will allow them to understand triumphs and tragedies, stupidity and brilliance, prejudice and compassion—in literature and in life. They will find their values being questioned—and affirmed. Literature will help them to see themselves.

In teaching literature, familiarity does not breed contempt. The most effective lessons in my classroom have been those where students have made some connection between the literary piece and something in their lives. This link may occur with a simple comment or question, or it may take up the entire period.

To illustrate the connections my students have made with classic literature, I offer the following descriptions of student activity and response.

Fatal Attraction: *Medea*

A student's comment triggered this exercise. One year, when we were studying *Medea*, a student found Medea's actions to be unbelievable: "No one's that obsessed." At the time, *Fatal Attraction* was number one at the box office, and *Time* and *People* had both come out with cover stories that provided a plethora of examples of contemporary, real-life, fatal attractions. I brought in examples of obsession-related revenge behavior, as well. The students' favorite was that of an inventive young lady who had been asked to move out of her boyfriend's apartment. He was leaving for the weekend and wanted her out by the time he returned Sunday night. Upon his return, he was afraid of what he might find; he did not notice anything, until he saw that his phone was off the hook. He picked up the receiver . . . and discovered he was listening to the time recording in Tokyo. This and other examples inspired students to write about their own revenge techniques, as well as situations in which they, or those they knew, were cruelly dumped by a boyfriend or girlfriend. This exercise was done in class, anonymously, written on a half sheet of paper. Following are some sample rejections and revenge techniques:

> I bought two concert tickets ($20 apiece) and let her hold them. She dumped me and took her new boyfriend to the concert with my tickets.

> The cruelest dumping I know of happened to a friend of mine the night before homecoming. She had been dating a guy for over a year. They were very serious and had even talked of marriage. The night before homecoming, his mother called her mother and informed her that the boy never wanted to see her again.

> I took the classic revenge—I dated his best friend.

> This guy I know poured ten gallons of milk in his ex-girlfriend's car one night.

> I rolled his car with eight rolls of toilet paper on the outside and four inside, cellophaned the door handles, and then poured some water over the car, which froze, or course. If I had been really mean, I could have turned on the lights so the car wouldn't start, but I was too nice for that.

> I got back at her by putting sugar in her new boyfriend's gas tank.

Looking for Love: Greek Drama

Some students are very much aware of personal advertisements placed in local newspapers and magazines. They also notice that many of our Greek characters were not too lucky in love. In a "mini-assignment" to be turned in along with a full-fledged composition, students were asked to consider the situation of the characters in the Greek literature we had read, particularly how they had not done well in affairs of the heart. Students were asked either to write an advertisement which one of the characters might have placed, considering his or her fate, or to help out the character by writing the ad the character *should* have placed. Some of the results follow:

> Looking for a girl just like the one who married dear old dad. (Oedipus)

Newcomer to Thebes. At a crossroad in my life and am seeking companionship. Am blinded by the beauty of older women. If you're not afraid to broach the subject of love, call Ed. (Oedipus)

Me: Well-traveled, good position.
You: Sharp, high-powered.
We: Will enjoy snuggling on tapestries and taking sensuous baths. (Agamemnon)

Looking for a mate. No children, please. (Aegisthus)

The Power of Music: Dryden's "A Song for St. Cecilia's Day"

After reading Dryden's "A Song for St. Cecilia's Day," we talked about the power of music. I asked the students to write about a song that felt powerful to them in some way; it could evoke a memory (positive or negative), or inspire them to want to get up and dance, or evoke a certain mood. I had them take out a half sheet of paper, and after they finished writing, I collected the sheets and read them aloud, anonymously:

"I Can't Drive 55" reminds me of totaling my dad's car.

"All at Once" reminds me of a very special guy I lost in a drunk-driver car accident. Every time I hear it, I burst into tears.

The song "Something So Strong" reminds me of going to a work camp in Michigan where we rebuilt or repaired houses for the elderly. A guy I met there was singing it, and it makes me think of how much it meant to help other people. It makes me feel good—the way I felt then.

"Don't Rain on My Parade" is a great song for me. It raises my spirits and helps me to remember not to let life get me down. There's a particular line that says, "Hey, world, here I am." Some day the world will look at me, and they will be amazed at what they see.

"Find a Way" was my sister's favorite song, and it described her personality. It means a lot to me because of what she accomplished while she was sick. A verse of it was read for her eulogy.

No Person Is an Island: John Donne's "Meditation XVII"

While studying Donne's "Meditation XVII," we looked at the line "no man is an island," and we determined whether or not we agreed with that. I posed the following question to the class: "Do we really feel anything when people unknown to us die in an earthquake on the other side of the world? Why or why not?" After a brief discussion, I asked them to respond to the following question: "Can you think of any situations where you did not know the people involved, yet you either rejoiced with them in the triumph or sympathized with them in their tragedy?" The students felt that they had shared feelings of elation with the family and rescuers of Baby Jessica; with their favorite sports teams, upon winning a championship; with the rescuers of the whales in Alaska. The overwhelming example of shared tragedy was the explosion of the *Challenger* space shuttle and especially the death of Christa McAuliffe. Playing the devil's advocate, I said, "Why did that bother you? You didn't know her." Inevitably, a student responded with, "She was a teacher, a wife, a mother—people with whom we can identify—that we know and love."

Back to the Future: *Beowulf*

While studying *Beowulf*, we compared the typical Anglo-Saxon hero with heroes of today. We determined which of today's heroes would or would not survive if dropped into Anglo-Saxon society. I had the students list three people they considered to be heroes, giving reasons and predicting their "survivability" in Anglo-Saxon times. They speculated on what would surprise Beowulf were he in the twentieth century.

The big winners in the "herostakes" were Ronald Reagan and Superman; our arguments were most vehement over Oliver North and subway vigilante Bernhard Goetz. The students decided that Arnold Schwarzenegger, Rambo, Hulk Hogan, and Muhammad Ali would survive in Anglo-Saxon times because of their physical prowess; those who would not survive included Michael Jackson and Phil Donahue. According to the students, the following would have surprised Beowulf:

Intellectual capabilities are admired more than strength.

The advanced weaponry that has replaced physical combat; in order to do anything, one has to go through a lot of red tape.

Pacifists protesting war.

The lack of honesty in our society; a person's word doesn't necessarily mean anything.

The scorn of religion.

The nature of today's weapons; the position of women in society; and the slight, physical stature of today's leaders.

McDonald's.

The low quality of our beer.

A Poetic Pilgrimage: *The Canterbury Tales*

After reading the prologue to Chaucer's *The Canterbury Tales* and examining Chaucer's use of subtle detail and of objective, nonjudgmental viewpoint, I had the students write a modern-day version using Chaucer's technique. One student targeted the administration's dress code for students, along with the reasons behind the code:

> Cut-offs and sweats, of which the rule speaks,
> Are never allowed, not even the first three weeks.
> The sight of such articles is such a distraction,
> Especially when we learn to divide a complex fraction.
> Thank goodness for high school and its rules, for hence,
> In college we'll be burdened with independence.

Satiric Slams: *Gulliver's Travels*

After studying excerpts of political satire from Swift's *Gulliver's Travels,* we brought in examples of satiric editorial cartoons, as well as excerpts from *Doonesbury*. After we passed them around and discussed them, I had the students try their luck with satire. The following is one of those results:

WANTED: PRESIDENT

Prestigious employer seeking very available man. Applicant must have the face of a minister, the acting ability of an Academy Award winner, faith in a deity, and no distinct opinion on anything. Knowledge of finance or ability to balance a budget not required. Individual must also have many friends in high-ranking places with no idea how they got there. This aggressive individual must be able to dance very quickly without stepping on toes, and promote world peace while also promoting the Star Wars ideal. Candidates must realize Geneva is *not* a brand of sportswear, and USSR does *not* stand for Understanding Strategic Stockmarket Rhetoric. The applicant must hire loyal secretaries, and supply own paper shredder. A deep understanding of high-tech audio-visual equipment hidden in the Oval Office is also required.

The preceding examples show students finding something of their own lives in the lines of literary masterpieces, either applying the ideas of the classics to their times or projecting the present onto the circumstances of classic expressions. Even connections that might seem trivial on the surface come to loom large in these young lives. Let's help them find the connections.

17 On Teaching Poetry

Perry Oldham
Casady School, Oklahoma City, Oklahoma

How often have you heard English teachers, and not just rookies, fretting about teaching poetry, which they feel obliged to do, yet which they have only the vaguest notion of how to teach? Having once counted myself among their number, I would like to share some ideas for teaching poetry in a college-preparatory class. These practices have evolved over the past fifteen years, and over the past several years, they have produced remarkably successful results— by "success," I mean students who understand how poetry works and who are able to communicate this understanding competently.

The core of the approach lies in cultivating a student's ability to respond to the *experience* of the poem. I am convinced that trying to analyze a poem without having first experienced it is like trying to get at a novel through *Cliffs Notes*: both are shortcuts and hence, reductive, in that both oversimplify or reduce something of enormous, inherent complexity.

Taking as a point of departure Wallace Stevens's (1951) statement "that, above everything else, poetry is words; and that words, above everything else, are, in poetry, sounds," I suggest that the teacher normally begin by reading a poem aloud once or twice. Direct students not to worry about meaning at this point, but to just listen to the sounds. Then ask, "What does the poem *sound* like?" For example, the reeling, three-beat lines of William Carlos Williams's "The Dance" sound just like what they describe—a rollicking peasant dance. Tennyson's "Ulysses" sounds introspective and dignified. "Jabberwocky" sounds slashing and fanciful and exotic.

After sharing Williams's perception that a poem is a little machine in which each part fulfills an essential task—and in which there are no "spare parts"—I invite students to comment on particular comparisons or sound patterns or images by asking, "What is this doing? How is this working? What effect is achieved here?" even, "What is this saying?"

However, I avoid asking "What does this *mean*?" which tends to reduce the poem to a mere puzzle or ingenious code. Nor do I ask, "What is the poet *trying* to say?" which implies that if only the poet had had the skill to express himself or herself more clearly, there would not be a "problem." Students may find it illuminating to learn that good poetry is written as clearly as it can be written; the complexity of what is being transmitted, both to the emotions and to the intellect, is such that it cannot be expressed in simpler terms.

Only after treating the poem directly, in the experiential manner described above, do I adopt a more explicitly analytical approach. I now want to encourage the students to sharpen their perceptions of the poem by conceptualizing those perceptions. I also want to provide the students with an appropriate descriptive vocabulary that will give names to the ideas and devices they will be talking about.

For example, we read "To His Coy Mistress" and savor the irony of Marvell's acerbic "The grave's a fine and private place, / But none, I think, do there embrace." We analyze the enormous contrasts in tone among the poem's three sections and note how these contrasts reflect the argument. After providing them with a translation, I play Lotte Lenya's evocative recording of Brecht's cabaret song "Bills Ballhaus in Bilbao," and we observe how essential is the device of repetition, and particularly the alliterating, bouncing B's, to achieving the song's lilting, honky-tonk effect. We take apart sonnets by Shakespeare and perceive how the development of the thought is linked with the sonnet form; how the Italian sonnet of an eight-line group followed by a six-line group naturally lends itself to a statement of thesis, followed by a response, or antithesis; how the English sonnet of three quatrains followed by a couplet just as naturally invites three statements, followed by a comment or a resolution. Then we note that what we have been talking about is included under the categories of "structure" and "form."

If all goes well, after spending several, successive class periods examining poems in this informed manner, students will be better equipped to read a poem and respond to it, as well as to feel increasingly secure discussing it in appropriately sophisticated language.

When teaching a poetry unit, I normally lead discussion on the first day, to model the process of talking about a poem. Then, I distribute poems among the students, in preparation for each one to lead a discussion. (It's time for this poetry project to become their show.) Each student is then held responsible for reading his or her poem aloud in a smooth and effective manner, for getting the class to discover "how it works," and for pointing out anything else remarkable about it.

Of course, you accept a risk in conveying responsibility for the class discussion to the students. A few of them will manage to be absent when presentations are due; others will have "forgotten." Some interpretations may seem perversely wrongheaded, as when one dear-heart in my senior poetry class introduced the ingenuous notion that Emily Dickinson's "I felt a Funeral, in my Brain" is "about a headache." (In developing her interpretation, the student relied heavily on the lines "A Service, like a Drum— / Kept beating—beating—till I thought / My Mind was going numb . . .")

On such occasions, it is important to keep one's priorities straight. Certainly, one bears a responsibility to the text, to see what the words on the page mean, to read them accurately. But one also has a responsibility to be sensitive to the student's feelings and level of understanding. In order to master the difficult art of reading a poem, the student must be allowed to make honest mistakes, without fear of tactless censure or ridicule. Otherwise, there is little chance she will ever learn either to read *or* to love a poem. And so one nods encouragingly, and respectfully hears the student out. My own way of dealing with the "headache" reading was then to invite responses from others in the class. When antithetical interpretations were not forthcoming, I noted as tactfully as I could that "critics have suggested a different reading of the poem. . . ." Such a situation demands a difficult balancing act on the part of the teacher: preserving the integrity of the poem, while protecting the integrity of the student.

These, however, are worst-case scenarios. At their best, student-led discussions produce genuinely fresh and illuminating interpretations of poems that you have sometimes taught so many times that you've become deadened to them. In addition to setting a high standard for the class and dazzling them, these presentations may teach you something.

I conclude the poetry unit by giving students the opportunity to show what they have learned, by writing an in-class analysis of a poem they have not seen before. A good poem, a challenging poem, should be chosen for this purpose. For example, after spending a week on Emily Dickinson, my eleventh graders wrote on the following topic: "In a well-written paper, explicate 'I taste a liquor never brewed.' Pay particular attention to the poet's use of such elements as prosody, sound, metaphor and simile, symbolism, irony, diction, and imagery to convey her point." Or they might be asked to write a poem themselves, in imitation of a poem they've read—the sort of imaginative assignment developed by Kenneth Koch (1973) in his classic *Rose, Where Did You Get That Red?* If possible, I have them do both sorts of assignments, perhaps writing a poem first, in order to give them a look at poetry from the inside out, and subsequently moving into analysis. As is usually the case with effective teaching, variety of approach is important.

Finally, I would urge the teacher of poetry not only to retain, but to display, a sense of humor. I want to convey to my students that I take poetry quite personally and seriously—as in fact I do—yet that I am eager to laugh with them. This may take the form of an irreverent demonstration of the well-known fact that the hymn (or ballad) stanza—the stanza Emily Dickinson used for most of her poems—is also the stanza of "The Yellow Rose of Texas." It is that rare student who can resist laughing at the teacher warbling, "Because I could not stop for death" to the tune of "The Yellow Rose of Texas!" I don't think Dickinson would disapprove. Like all good poems, "Because I could not stop for death" is tough. But with the right spirit, on the part of readers, it comes through.

Works Cited

Koch, Kenneth. 1973. *Rose, Where Did You Get That Red?* New York: Vintage Books.

Stevens, Wallace. 1951. "The Noble Rider and the Sound of Words." In *The Necessary Angel: Essays on Reality and the Imagination*, 3–36. New York: Vintage Books.

18 Transcendentalists Run for President

Gary A. Watson
Butler Traditional/Technical High School, Louisville, Kentucky

American literature and high school juniors may not always be entirely compatible, especially when the literature is that of the Transcendental authors and thinkers. While I could envision my students shrinking from the dry words on the pages of the literature anthology, I thought they might react favorably to a "hands-on" study involving the thoughts and lives of the Transcendentalists.

The students were offered the opportunity to conduct a presidential election activity using the personae of various Transcendental authors (Thoreau, Emerson, Dickinson, Whitman, etc.) as candidates. After researching what the various authors believed and wrote and what kind of people they were, the students discussed their findings and made applications to current issues (opinions on war, pro-life and pro-choice, government spending, pacifism, etc.). Then they prepared campaign strategies for the author-candidates. Students chose authors to represent, made campaign plans, prepared campaign literature and posters, prepared speeches for class delivery, developed questions to ask each other, and wrote about their reactions to what the Transcendentalists stood for and what they believed they would stand for today.

On "Election Day" all candidate-authors and their campaign staffs decorated the walls of the classroom with posters and fliers. Each candidate-author was allowed time for a statement and mini-pep rally, and each had to answer questions from the "voters." Students dressed for their roles and, to the best of their ability, acted the roles of the various candidates. The candidate-authors talked about the actions and beliefs of their respective personae in terms of modern issues and concerns. After all the campaign activities, secret balloting produced the winner of the election. In our election, Emily Dickinson won.

Afterward, students discussed and wrote about their opinions and their feelings regarding the election and their reactions to the campaign. The students displayed a great deal of interest and enjoyment, and learned a great deal about their own beliefs in relation to the views of the Transcendentalists.

IV Merging the Disciplines

English and the language arts have not escaped the cycles of separation and union that have characterized academic disciplines within twentieth-century American education. After the narrow-interest, elective course era of a few years ago, it seems that we are well into another era of integration of the disciplines—and for good reasons, both theoretical and practical.

Within the English discipline, whole language approaches are bringing reading and writing instruction together with oral language activity. General English classes have returned to high school schedules. Across disciplines, integrated or unified studies draw upon several of the humanities or upon both social studies and English.

In addition to integration at the course level, we also find teachers' creative integration of several skills and areas of knowledge within the context of an idea or concept in carrying out the unit method. Instead of the language arts being the servant of a historic or social concept, each becomes an equal partner in an educational enterprise that aims at student growth and learning, rather than academic niceties.

Working in wholes and bringing together the disciplines to focus on unifying themes makes good sense, both psychologically and pedagogically. Learners do not make fine distinctions about subject-matter lines. Rather, they seek answers to their questions and benefit from the range of learning skills, wherever their search leads them. Language skills definitely make more sense when they are applied in the context of some meaningful engagement.

Here, we offer Myra Zarnowski's description of a unit called "Biography in Verse," which involves applications of historical research and the writing of poetry. Her sixth graders needed to utilize the circumstances in the life of a historic figure, the opportunity for original interpretation, and the poetic possibilities in the sounds and nuances of linguistic resources.

In William Mollineaux's "Booktalks," the integration is within

English, as students combine insightful reading, planned speech, and sales technique to enhance the literacy and literary levels of their seventh-grade classroom.

In his application of the cento—manifested here as a meaningful mosaic of poetic lines taken from published poems—G. Douglas Meyers demonstrates a rich, integrated reading-writing activity. Students read widely to fill a journal with quotable lines; then, they craft their own centos around an idea. The student samples are intriguing.

"The Year in Review," as designed by Ronald Barron, involves students in historical research, modeling of media methodology, and presentation of data in ways that require language, visuals, and costume, all accomplished as a group enterprise.

19 Biography in Verse

Myra Zarnowski
Queens College, CUNY

Poetry, history, and writing may seem, at first glance, to be the makings of a "pedagogical" Molotov cocktail—guaranteed to bomb. However, experience has taught me that students develop an appreciation of all three subjects under similar classroom conditions: having large chunks of time devoted to (1) investigating these subjects in all their complexity; (2) creating a product based on current understandings; and (3) sharing their thoughts about process and product.

Last year, sixth-grade teacher Lila Alexander and I combined the study of poetry, history, and writing during several months of focused workshop activity in her classroom. We challenged sixth graders to create original poetry picture books about well-known historical figures, while at the same time providing the time, materials, and support for getting the job done. This essay will consider briefly *why* this procedure was developed and then explain *how* it was implemented.

Teaching Poetry, History, and Writing Together

There is an obvious benefit to teaching three subjects at the same time—no small consideration for teachers faced with an "elastic" curriculum that is continuously being stretched to include more. But beyond this time-saving feature, the trio of poetry, history, and writing forms a mutually supportive network.

Together, these three subjects provide one with a complex set of ideas to think about. *Poetry* draws students' attention to language—to the use of sound and carefully chosen words and phrases. *History* provides intriguing content. Who did what? Why? How? When? Where? What does it mean to be a discoverer? An explorer? A prodigy? A leader in the face of overwhelming odds? How do some people manage to push the limits? A focus on individual stories introduces students to the larger historical context in which the story took place. *Writing* an original interpretation of historical events enables students to leave a personal imprint on material they have studied. In the process of "doing" history—transforming "the facts" in original ways—students claim the past as their own. As an added bonus, they are left with a product that can be shared, debated, and even revised.

Guiding Children to Write Biography in Verse

Lila Alexander and I share a continuing interest in teaching history through reading-and-writing approaches. Our goal is to enable students to interpret history for themselves, not to see it as a collection of inert facts; that is why we have become enthusiastic about the growing library of student-produced, poetry picture books that tell about the lives of real people. After reading a number of these books, children can adopt this format for their own purposes.

We have used poetry picture books about people both as sources of enjoyment and as models for children's writing. The long-range challenge we posed for children was to write an original poetry picture book about a historical figure. The challenge we posed for ourselves was to support the children's efforts with a combination of teaching, listening, coaching, and staying out of the way. The steps we followed are described below.

Examining Poetry Picture Books Featuring People

Quite a number of poetry picture books tell about actual people. Some of the titles we have used are included in the list of recommended reading at the end of this chapter. These books and others were read aloud and made available for the children's perusal. Following each reading, Lila and I held focused class discussions. First, we asked children to consider the poetry picture books in relation to other types of nonfiction. We posed the following questions: How is this book similar to other nonfiction books? How is it different? The children responded by mentioning structural similarities such as the use of a title page, introduction, foreword, and afterword. They also pointed out the informative nature of nonfiction books and the fact that these books often highlighted people's accomplishments.

When asked about differences, the children spent considerable time discussing the fact that poetry picture books usually focused on one aspect of the person's life rather than "telling it all." They also noted the rhyme scheme found in some books, the poetic language, and the close connection between illustration and text. Several children commented that some poems were told in the first person, from the subject's point of view. A chart listing these similarities and differences was compiled and displayed in the classroom.

A second discussion topic was the language found in the various poems. Lila and I asked the class to listen for words and phrases that were interesting, unusual, or even confusing. We noted these words and phrases, and then together we worked on "translating" them into conversational language. For example, Longfellow's phrase, "a glimmer and then a gleam of light," found in *Paul Revere's Ride,* was translated into the more colloquial "first a small amount of light, then a bright light." This very useful procedure (Denman 1988) enabled children to bring up confusing or interesting phrases that they wanted to discuss, and prevented Lila and me from overanalyzing and dissecting a poem.

Researching People to Write About

After a few weeks of looking at poetry picture books, the class selected historical figures to research and to write about. Children formed research groups so that they could then share insights, questions, and opinions about their subject. We selected the following subjects: Christopher Columbus, Mozart, Mary McLeod Bethune, Sitting Bull, and Golda Meir. This diverse group would—in fact, did—open the door to many controversial discussions. Was Mozart unfairly exploited by his father? Was Columbus a hero? Did Bethune teach the right things?

Knowing from the start that they would be using their knowledge to write poetry picture books, the children kept journals in which they wrote down the facts they wanted to remember, their responses to what they read, and questions they wanted to answer. At the beginning of the study of Christopher Columbus, one child wrote:

> Today in my book I read that Christopher Columbus sent a letter to the King and Queen saying that he found islands and named them. . . . Do any of the islands still have the names that Columbus gave them?

The children read, wrote journal entries, and met with their groups for several weeks of intensive research. Then each child began to plan and write an original poetry picture book.

Writing Biography in Verse

As the children began to write, they carefully examined published books to discover such things as how the authors divided and punctuated their lines, whether or not they used rhyme, and how they integrated work and illustration. The class decided that their books would have the following parts: cover, title page, copyright, dedication, text and pictures, and information about the author. However, it was up to each author to decide which aspect(s) of the person's life to highlight, what to say, and what illustrations to add.

A number of children chose to have the subject of the poem do the narrating, as in this poem about Mozart:

Wolfgang Amadeus Mozart: The Genius

I am Wolfgang Amadeus Mozart,
    who thrilled the ears of the world,
I have been dragged all over Europe
    to sing and to play,
I am going to tell you that story today.

It all started out like this,
    When my father held up his fist,
And exclaimed, "I have two wonder children
    for all the world to see!"

This was the day when all the traveling started,
    The first day was to Munich,
What a long ride it was.
I asked my father, "When will we be there?"
    He was always taking me wherever he wanted,
And this was not fair.

The next day was to Vienna,
    To play for Queen Theresa.
My jaws just dropped open when I
    saw the king's palace,
Wow, what a beautiful palace I did see,
    I really wish that palace
    belonged to me.

Some people said that I had golden hands,
    Others said I was a genius,
But I thought it all meant the same.
When people said that I was a fake,
    That got me mad,
It made me lose the power of music I had.

When people asked me,
    "Which tour was your best?"
I said, "The Grand Tour, of course."

That journey started from the desert land,
  Through all the burning rocks and sand,
That day was really hot,
    don't you see
That was the hottest day there will ever be.

The desert was very dry,
I wished one drop of water
would drop from the sky.

I am Wolfgang Amadeus Mozart,
  Who filled the air with music
  and peace everywhere.
I hope the musical world will last
  from today until tomorrow!

This poem takes the position that while Mozart was a genius "who thrilled the ears of the world," he was also unfairly "dragged all over Europe." Other poems about Mozart echoed this position. One child wrote that "Wolfgang's life was like being in prison," but in the same poem, remarked that he "was a wonder, a light."

Conclusion

Writing biography in verse was a challenging yet manageable project for sixth-grade students. They were asked to apply what they had learned from reading, writing, and speaking with others in order to create something new—a biography told in verse. Students were asked to transform material and to tell things in a manner that reflected their own ideas.

At the same time, this project was manageable because there was sufficient time to research a topic, discuss it with others, and write about it for extended periods of time. In addition, students knew that they were free to focus on one aspect of the person's life without having to tell the entire story. Viewed this way, poetry picture books became a friendly format for our sixth-grade poet-biographers.

Work Cited

Denman, G. A. 1988. *When You've Made It Your Own*: *Teaching Poetry to Young People*. Portsmouth, NH: Heinemann.

Recommended Reading

Benét, Stephen Vincent. 1959. *The Ballad of William Sycamore*. Illustratedby Brinton Turkle. Boston: Little, Brown.

Lindbergh, Reeve. 1990. *Johnny Appleseed.* Illustrated by Kathy Jakobsen. Boston: Joy Street/Little, Brown.

Longfellow, Henry Wadsworth. 1983. *Hiawatha.* Illustrated by Susan Jeffers. New York: Dial.

———. 1990. *Paul Revere's Ride.* Illustrated by Ted Rand. New York: Dutton.

Merriam, Eve. 1968. *Independent Voices.* Illustrated by Arvis Stewart. New York: Atheneum.

Swift, Hildegarde Hoyt. 1947. *North Star Shining: A Pictorial History of the American Negro.* Illustrated by Lynd Ward. New York: Morrow.

20 Booktalks: Leave Them to the Students

William R. Mollineaux
Sedgwick Middle School, West Hartford, Connecticut

"Boy, Mr. M., I couldn't put down Avi's *Wolf Rider!*" exclaimed an excited Rob. "I kept hoping that Andy would be able to get someone to believe him that Zeke was serious about killing Nina. Do you have any other books by Avi? Is there another book like *Wolf Rider?* You know, one that makes you feel like you're part of the story?"

"And I just couldn't stop reading Spinelli's *Maniac Magee!*" bubbled Sarah. "I liked the way it ended. I was surprised that Maniac didn't wind up living with the Pickwells, but he did wind up with a real home. Guess we all need that, don't we?"

Unfortunately, the sound of the bell ending the period prevented us from unleashing a myriad of questions. As I drove home that evening, I continued to reflect on how and why these two average readers became so involved with these two novels. What had happened to cause Rob and Sarah to become so enthusiastic, so insightful about their reading? Could it be . . . ? Yeah, that's it! *Booktalks!*

At the end of last year, I was disappointed that my seventh graders were not reading as much as I had expected, especially since over five hundred young adult paperbacks filled the bookshelves in my classroom. Realizing that I had not introduced this literature to my students in a systematic, stimulating manner, I became determined to rectify the situation. Consequently, that summer I read, reread, and skimmed as many young adult novels as possible, including all genres and reading levels. Science fiction, mystery, romance, fantasy, poetry, adventure, and nonfiction—all became part of my daily reading diet.

By the time school began in the fall, I had become even more familiar with a lot of good books and felt confident that I could successfully steer my students toward books they would enjoy. To help implement this goal, I decided to give frequent booktalks each week, focusing on variety. That this approach worked is evidenced by the comments Rob and Sarah made. And as I continued thinking

about it, every one of the books I talked about had been read and
enjoyed by at least one student.

Good! It worked. But like any other teacher, I was not satisfied.
There must be a way to get the students more involved. Realizing
that my students selected their reading from two major sources—their
friends and my booktalks—I wondered if there wasn't a way to
combine them. The answer quickly, and almost too simply, emerged:
Have the students give booktalks!

Have the students give booktalks? At first this appeared to be
just like the usual oral book reports that both students and teachers
find excruciatingly dull. But that wasn't the way I had given my
booktalks, nor the reaction that they'd received. Instead of talking for
a full period and trying to cram in as many book reports as possible,
I had discussed only one book for about five to ten minutes at the
beginning of a period.

By now my students had a good idea of what a booktalk could
be. Before initiating my new plan, however, I felt that I must consciously
model several more booktalks, concentrating on ways to make a book
appealing. I made sure that I included a "Sweet Valley High" selection,
as well as books by Christopher Pike, R. L. Stine, Lois Duncan, Robert
Cormier, Richard Peck, Walter Dean Myers, Paula Danziger, Susan
Cooper, Jay Bennett, Katherine Paterson, and Gary Paulsen. I was
striving for variety, and I also wanted to capitalize on what I knew
students really enjoyed reading. In other words, by including "Sweet
Valley High," Pike, and Stine, I was showing the students that I was
familiar with the kinds of books that appealed to them and that I
respected their choices. By acknowledging these realities, I believed
that they, in turn, would be receptive to more varied and demanding
options.

Before giving a booktalk, I carefully rehearsed what I wanted
to say about the book—why I really enjoyed it and why I thought
others might enjoy it, too. Usually, I showed the book to the students
(so they would be able to recognize the cover), I gave a brief synopsis
of the plot, and then I elaborated on things that I enjoyed about the
book—things that made it special for me. For example, Agatha
Christie's *And Then There Were None* was special because of the island
setting, the nursery rhyme that described the method of each murder,
and the suspense of wondering who was going to be the next victim.
Additionally, I read one or more excerpts from the book to get the
students accustomed to the author's style, and to grab their interest
with some effective passages. All I had to do was read the first two

pages in Avi's *Wolf Rider* or some of chapter 8 in Annette Curtis Klause's *The Silver Kiss,* and they were hooked. Also, because students enjoy knowing something about an author's personal life, I shared biographical information from Don Gallo's *Speaking for Ourselves* (1990) and Kenneth Donelson and Alleen Nilsen's *Literature for Today's Young Adults* (1989).

Although I felt that modeling was absolutely essential in showing what I expected a booktalk to be, I also believed that for student booktalks to be successful, the students had to really think about what went into a booktalk. To accomplish this, I asked the students to discuss in small groups of three or four what they thought the criteria of a booktalk should be. Then, in a large-group discussion, the students refined, honed, and finalized *their list.* I emphasize "their list" because it had to be the students' if the booktalks were going to be successful. This was no teacher-imposed set of criteria. They knew what they wanted to discuss in a booktalk, and what they deemed important to hear when listening to one. In fact, their criteria exceeded mine in completeness and was, by far, more demanding. The criteria included:

1. Was biographical information included?
2. Was the length of the talk between five and ten minutes?
3. Was the presenter enthusiastic?
4. Was the presenter convincing?
5. Did the selections that were read aloud support the presenter's views?
6. Was the presenter prepared?

But the main thing was that they knew it was theirs.

Now we were ready to begin. Many students volunteered to go first; others were hesitant, so we introduced a lottery system for them. Providing an adequate number of selections for the booktalks was not the problem I thought it would be. My booktalks had made them aware of many authors. When they liked one book by an author, they often would choose another by the same author.

However, to help students select books, I had in my room copies of *Books for You* and *Your Reading,* both of which are published regularly by NCTE, each containing approximately 2,000 entries that are annotated and categorized. Additionally, periodicals that I subscribe to— *The ALAN Revue, The New Advocate, Horn Book,* and *Voya*—were available for the students. Some of the most popular titles were Bennett's *The Skeleton Man,* Duncan's *Summer of Fear,* Sebestyen's *The Girl in the Box,* Sleator's *The Duplicate,* and White's *Deathwatch.*

After students had presented their booktalks, I gave them a copy of the class's criteria for a booktalk and had them evaluate their own presentations. Thus, the students were given time to reflect on their booktalks, using the criteria that they had helped to establish. The next day, in a short conference, each student and I reviewed his or her self-evaluation. Here, I tried to keep quiet and let the student do the talking. Invariably, the students were harder on themselves than I would have been, each making observations about the presentation that reflected considerable insight.

If you have to worry about grades, as I must, this procedure makes things much easier, especially since the student is doing the really difficult task: evaluation. As with the booktalks, I have modeled this conference with the students. They know what is expected, and once again the task has been made easier—after all, it is *their* criteria. When, and if, a student's evaluation is unrealistic (either too positive or too negative), a few questions from me, based on the established criteria, will usually set things right.

After all of the students had completed their booktalks, they returned to their original small groups and evaluated what had taken place during the last month. Their conclusions extended even what I had hoped for. Besides discovering new and exciting books, the students enjoyed the informal, relaxed manner they had devised for giving a booktalk. For them, it was a rewarding, enjoyable experience that was worth their effort; for me, it was a dream come true—students talking intelligently about books and clamoring to read more.

This approach has created not only a literary atmosphere in my classroom, but a viable means for getting my seventh graders to read more. It has also provided a way for students to become aware of books that are available and to become more involved with the literature that they read. Fortunately, for my students, I had the faith in them to try it!

Works Cited

Donelson, Kenneth L., and Alleen Pace Nilsen, eds. 1989. *Literature for Today's Young Adults*. 3rd ed. Glenview, IL: Scott, Foresman.

Gallo, Don, comp. and ed. 1990. *Speaking for Ourselves: Autobiographical Sketches by Notable Authors of Books for Young Adults*. Urbana: NCTE.

21 Connecting Content and Context through the Cento

G. Douglas Meyers
University of Texas at El Paso

A cento is any literary work made up of parts of other literary works. Centones (the plural form) are not limited to any single genre, but the word "cento," as used in this article, is limited to poetry, specifically describing a kind of poem that is composed as a patchwork of lines originally written by different poets. The cento has a rich heritage, and two noteworthy masterpieces that possess elements of it are T. S. Eliot's "The Waste Land" and Ezra Pound's *Cantos.* To engage students in authoring the cento, then, is to invite them to become members of a distinguished literary community.

It is also to affirm their roles as active meaning-makers—learners who construct and reconstruct meaning by interacting with others' poems and by writing their own. The cento assignment is firmly grounded in the principle that "omnivorous reading is certainly the best possible preparation for a student writer" (Minot 1989, 89), for writing a cento requires extensive reading as a prewriting activity. Facilitating the reading-writing connection is something that has received increased attention in our profession, as we realize how linking instruction in reading and writing helps students to master these reciprocal processes and to make crossovers between them (Dyson 1989; Tway 1985).

At the heart of the cento assignment is the conviction that both the reading and writing of poetry should be primarily *literary* experiences. The cento assignment is thus not "about" literature; instead, it values literature as "something through which we come to know" (Probst 1988, 20). By affirming that "the value of poetry is our response to it . . ." (Boyd 1973, 2), the cento assignment places itself solidly within the framework of a response-centered curriculum in which one response to reading poetry is writing it.

The essential activities that students undertake to write a cento are these: (1) reading poems from a variety of texts—textbooks, magazines, literature anthologies, collected works of single poets, etc.; (2) keeping a poetry notebook in which they (a) record lines of poetry which they like and (b) note the original source of each line; (3) composing (drafting and revising) their own original poems, using the contents of their poetry notebook; and (4) sharing their poems. The rationale underlying this sequence is that while most students may not feel they have the flair to write poetically, they can certainly recognize what they like in poems, and a poetry notebook serves as an excellent source book for the cento. Usually, certain lines of poetry are enjoyed because of the magical content they create in the context where they originally appear. A good deal of the fun (i.e., the learning) of writing a cento is removing these lines from their original contexts and creating, in a novel cento, some new interanimation among the lines.

Here, for instance, is a cento written using the poetry found in a literature textbook that has been adopted in our local schools:

Spring[1]

Greatly shining,
Breathless with adoration,
Spring is like a perhaps hand
Remembering, with twinklings and twinges.

It is in the small things we see
This living hand, now warm and capable.
Night after night her purple traffic
Strews the landing with Opal Bales
Like pure water
Touching clear sky,
Like the tipping
Of an object toward the light.

in Just—
Spring
Rough winds do shake the darling buds of May
The lone and level sands stretch far away
Yet knowing how way leads on to way

The poetry of earth is never dead.

The cento's closest relation in poetic discourse is "found poetry," poetry composed of texts that have been lifted out of *nonliterary* sources (Drake 1983, 68). In fact, using snippets of prose from newspapers and magazines (or song lyrics) to write found poems is a confidence-building warm-up to cento writing for students who may initially find "real" poetry too intimidating to borrow from; the cento and the found poem share a common power for raising awareness of what may be material for poetry (nearly anything!) and of how to break a line of free verse.

Writing the cento allows students to grapple with formal concerns in a way that encourages them to experiment with the elasticity of language, manipulating lines by placing them in certain locations and permuting them in a process of revision that reveals itself to be a recursive activity for discovering and refining one's intentions as a writer. As readers, cento writers also grow, expanding their repertoire of strategies for engaging with texts. Quite simply, the cento assignment helps students to achieve a poetic stature by strengthening the two faculties of poetry writing—craft and consciousness (Johnson 1990, 49).

The following three poems, the first two by my students and the third, my own, show the variety of ways in which centones may be written. The students' poems borrow from diverse sources and reflect their special interests in the poetry of Native Americans and women and in poetry written in Spanish (note the bilingual element in the second); mine, on the other hand, reflects my special admiration for one particular poet and draws exclusively on his work.

Re-rooting[2]

Yesterday it seemed
I saw for an instant what life is:
Voices and laughter, dancing and tambourines.
What once was in us now is not.
Too much hurt we have done to each other
And so many things I want to forget.
Why waste time knowing the husks of silence?
I require but my freedom, my passion's humanity.
I must not allow myself to disappear
Not yet, not yet—
I have no choice but to live.

A Cento[3]

Rise up, woman
Her eyes streaming with tears
Sorrow happens, hardship happens
You must always remember me
La Poderosa muerte me invitó muchas veces
Where might there be a refuge for me
And the air came in with lemon blossom fingers
Sending my spirit north, south, east and west.

Homage to Auden[4]

The uncomplaining stars compose their lucid song,
   Embrace and encourage each other
   In a brief moment of intersection.
Protected by the wide peace of the sun, the planets
   continue their circulation.
It is their tomorrow hangs over the earth of the living
   And all that we wish for our friends: but existence is
   believing
   We know for whom we mourn and who is grieving.
Little upon his little earth, man contemplates
   In a coma of waiting, just breathing.

Love like Matter is much
Odder than we thought.

The real unlucky dove
(His gift for magic made him chief
Of all those boyish powers of the air)
Must smarting fall away from brightness
Its love from living.

What does the song hope for?

While these three are more or less thematically organized, centones may also be based in images, sounds, rhythm, meter, and even nonsense. And while all of these have been individually authored, cento writing is fertile ground for group work—one poem being written collaboratively by a group of students, using lines that each group member has contributed.

The cento assignment is also a superb vehicle for making connections with other art forms whose aesthetic is based upon the synthesizing of parts from other works. In graphic arts, the collage can be used; in folk art, the quilt; in music, the pastiche; in television, the MTV video; and in film, the montage. Studying or creating in any of these media makes for superb "extension" exercises into the humanities.

Fundamentally, though, writing a cento is a lesson in the dynamics of language, contributing to students' understanding about epistemological issues of meaning and context, of revision, and of the inseparability of form and content. It also teaches lifelong lessons about ownership, for in "owning" others' poems in their own poems, students who write centones become empowered entrepreneurs in an exciting literary enterprise.

At a time when English teachers are simultaneously interested in connecting reading and writing and in enhancing students' responses to literature, the cento assignment can accomplish much. While it may originate as a teacher's assignment, its focus is really a fresh "uncommonsense" one (Mayher 1990, 215)—not so much on a teacher's teaching, but on the students' learning. And if it is true that "the artist brings order by altering perception" (Drake 1983, 85), then the cento assignment creates classrooms inhabited by artists: students whose poetry changes the way the world is experienced and teachers whose pedagogy changes the way students see themselves.

Notes

1. The sources, by line, are from the following poems: (1) A. Lowell, "Wind and Silver"; (2) W. Wordsworth, "It Is a Beauteous Evening"; (3) e. e. cummings, "Spring is like a perhaps hand"; (4) G. Brooks, "The Bean Eaters"; (5) A. Sexton, "Courage"; (6) J. Keats, "Lines Supposed to Have Been Written to Fanny Brawne"; (7) and (8) E. Dickinson, "This Is the Land the Sunset Washes"; (9) and (10) R. Brautigan, "All Watched Over by Machines of Loving Grace"; (11) and (12) E. Bishop, "The Fish"; (13) and (14) e. e. cummings, "in Just-"; (15) W. Shakespeare, "Shall I Compare Thee to a Summer's Day?"; (16) P. B. Shelley, "Ozymandius"; (17) R. Frost, "The Road Not Taken"; (18) J. Keats, "On the Grasshopper and Cricket."

2. The title is from D. Levertov's "Re-rooting." The sources, by line, are as follows: 1 - P. Neruda, "Ode to Laziness"; 2 - O. Paz, "The Balcony"; 3 - O. Paz, "Solo for Two Voices"; 4 - F. Garcia-Lorca, "Unsleeping City"; 5 - D. Levertov, "Beginners"; 6 - P. Neruda, "Autumn Testament"; 7 - P. Neruda, "Furies and Sufferings"; 8 - F. Garcia-Lorca, "Double Poem of Lake Eden"; 9 - P. Neruda, "We Are Many"; 10 - D. Levertov, "Beginners"; 11 - P. Neruda, "The Builder."

3. The sources, by line, are from the following: (1) Ayacucho Indian Song; (2) Y. Yevtushenko, "Weddings"; (3) Y. Yevtushenko, "Lies"; (4) Santo Domingo Indian Song; (5) P. Neruda, "The Heights of Macchu Picchu" (translates as "Irresistible death invited me many times"); (6) M. Moore, "Tell Me, Tell Me"; (7) P. Neruda, "The Heights of Macchu Picchu"; (8) Luiseño Indian Song.

4. The sources, by line, are the following poems by W. H. Auden: (1) "Voltaire at Ferney"; (2) and (3) "Autumn 1940"; (4) and (5) "Commentary"; (6) through (9) "In Memory of Ernst Toller"; (10) "Commentary"; (11) Autumn 1940"; (12) and (13) "Heavy Date"; (14) "The Decoys"; (15) and (16) "The First Temptation"; (17) and (18) "The Decoys"; (19) "Orpheus."

Works Cited

Boyd, Gertrude A. 1973. *Teaching Poetry in the Elementary School.* Columbus, OH: Merrill.

Drake, Barbara. 1983. *Writing Poetry.* New York: Harcourt Brace Jovanovich.

Dyson, Anne Haas, ed. 1989. *Collaboration through Writing and Reading: Exploring Possibilities.* Urbana: NCTE.

Johnson, David M. 1990. *Word Weaving: A Creative Approach to Teaching and Writing Poetry.* Urbana: NCTE.

Mayher, John S. 1990. *Uncommon Sense: Theoretical Practice in Language Education.* Portsmouth, NH: Boynton/Cook.

Minot, Stephen. 1989. "How a Writer Reads." In *Creative Writing in America: Theory and Pedagogy,* edited by Joseph M. Moxley, 89–95. Urbana: NCTE.

Probst, Robert E. 1988. "Readers and Literary Texts." In *Literature in the Classroom: Readers, Texts, and Contexts,* edited by Ben F. Nelms, 19–29. Urbana: NCTE.

Tway, Eileen. 1985. *Writing Is Reading: Twenty-Six Ways to Connect.* Urbana: ERIC/RCS and NCTE.

22 The Year in Review

Ronald Barron
Richfield High School, Richfield, Minnesota

Necessity has been called the mother of invention. The creation of my "1970s Year in Review" assignment attests to that observation. After listening, year after year, to my eleventh-grade students give speeches on some of the same old subjects, I knew I faced three possible alternatives: quit assigning informative or persuasive speeches, tolerate some of the old standbys but hope for a few original ones each year, or restructure the assignment.

On January 1, 1989, while watching one of the television networks recap the highlights of 1988, I realized that the format could be adapted to an assignment requiring groups of students to do research that they could present in the form of a year-end television broadcast. Thus was born the "1970s Year in Review" assignment, which I first had students do in the spring of 1989. The initial results were positive enough so that I have used a refined version of the assignment in subsequent years. Not only has the assignment helped preserve my mental health, and provided students with an opportunity to practice both speaking and research skills, but it has also provided the added side benefits of teaching students to work collaboratively and of providing them with an avenue for developing their creativity.

For this assignment, groups of students research, write, and dramatize a presentation that highlights the major events from one year in the decade of the 1970s. Why the 1970s? Because students have to do research to have something to say, rather than relying on what they know or think they already know, which might be the case if I allowed them to use a year from the 1980s. The activity also prevents students from recycling canned presentations on topics such as capital punishment, abortion, and nuclear disarmament, which they have already done to death.

Once they finish their research, students create a television newscast which might be broadcast on New Year's Day to review the preceding year. What the skits look like and how elaborate they are depend on two factors: the amount of research the students in the group have done and how creative the group members are in designing their presentations. Actually, the assignment has only three absolute requirements: the skit must contain sufficient factual material to indicate that group members have adequately researched the topic; the skit must be at least twenty minutes in length; and the skit must include speaking parts for all members of the group.

After I explain the nature of the assignment, students form groups of four to five people. I suggest they form mixed groups rather than unisex groups, since mixed groups usually find it easier to allocate the parts of the task. I write the years from 1970 to 1979 on individual slips of paper, and one member from each group draws a slip that indicates the year the group will use for its project.

Groups start their research by examining the two pages from *The Timetables of American History* (Urdang 1981) devoted to their assigned year. *The Timetables of American History* allocates two pages to each of the years from the twentieth century, with less extensive coverage devoted to the years from A.D. 1000 to A.D. 1900. These pages list briefly the highlights of the year for the United States and the world in four categories: History and Politics, The Arts, Science and Technology, and Miscellaneous. This book, or some book similar to it, is indispensable as a starting point because it provides students with a quick overview of the events they should consider including in their skits. *An Album of the Seventies* (Hoobler and Hoobler 1981) and *Day by Day: The Seventies* (Leonard, Crippen, and Aronson 1988) are two other sources that groups find useful while working on this project. Since both of these books are more detailed than *The Timetables of American History*, students usually find them more valuable after they start researching their portions of the script. Students are also given a bibliography of reference books which they may find helpful in completing the assignment. (Working with the media center director at their high school, teachers should be able to assemble a bibliography of reference books available in their media center which would be useful to students working on this project.) Some groups have also found encyclopedia yearbooks useful since they provide an overview of the year's major events. Finally, I urge members of the group to discuss the project with their parents, relatives, and neighbors to get some idea about what those people remember as being important for that particular year. All of these sources allow students to develop a list of items that they should incorporate into their presentations.

Students divide up roles for their newscast, a task which also gives each person a definite research responsibility. A key decision for the groups is the selection of their anchor person(s), the person(s) who will have the responsibility for providing transitional material to connect the individual segments of the newscast and also for presenting world news. Other typical roles include a commentator for state and local news, a sportscaster, and an entertainment reporter. However, these categories are merely suggestions. The type of special correspondents a group uses is determined by the significant events that occurred during their year, as well as by how elaborate they decide to make their newscast and what the group's particular interests are.

Once students have used the material from *The Timetables of American History,* the next logical step is to move on to newspapers and general news magazines such as *Time, Newsweek,* and *U.S. News & World Report.* Sportscasters, however, may find their best source material in back issues of *Sports Illustrated.* The media center in my high school has *Time* and *Newsweek* for the 1970s on microfiche, but for *Sports Illustrated* and for newspapers, my students have to consult one of the local public libraries. This is an added benefit to the assignment because students gain some familiarity with libraries other than the one in their own high school.

At this point in the project, I insert a lesson on how to use newspaper indexes and periodical indexes such as the *Reader's Guide to Periodical Literature.* Rather than appearing to be useless, this material suddenly has immediate, practical value to students because it enables them to quickly locate the information they need. The newspaper and magazine articles not only provide the detailed information they need to flesh out their portion of the script, but they also give them insight into how people and events were viewed during the 1970s, thus allowing the students to add authenticity to their skits.

Students devote several class periods to locating material, taking notes, and writing a preliminary version of their portion of the script. In most cases, however, students have to do additional work outside of class to complete this phase of the assignment. Some groups start the research phase by working independently, but while searching for material, they usually come across articles that might be of value to other members of the group; they realize that helping the others will improve the overall quality of their group's presentation. The groups recognize the benefits of working cooperatively and spend most of their research time in collaborative work. Some groups even plan to meet at neighborhood libraries in the evening or on weekends to work on their projects.

While students are conducting their research, I suggest that they watch real newscasts to learn how television stations cover stories. For example, how much time do they devote to each story and how do they use visual aids to supplement or complement what is being said? Occasionally, groups have taken on the roles of real newscasters and tried to duplicate their personal style.

Group members write a complete first draft of their scripts, and then they work collaboratively as a peer-response group to polish the material and to connect the individual parts. Further revision of their scripts occurs once the groups start to practice their presentations, because they get a sense of what works and what doesn't. Students are willing to make changes during the practice phase because they do not have to memorize their scripts, just as real newscasters do not memorize theirs. Last year, members of one innovative group had their complete script written in large letters on a continuous roll of paper, which they used like a teleprompter so group members could maintain eye contact with the audience while their skit was in progress.

This is the point in the process where individuals with specialized skills and interests contribute whatever they can that will be most helpful to the groups en masse. Also, at this point, groups consider methods to enliven their scripts to make them more interesting to the other students. For example, most groups present part of their skits as interviews, thus providing variety in their presentations. Some groups videotape portions of their scripts so that certain parts can be run like film taken on location. This technique allows group members to easily play multiple roles in the skit. Deciding to use visual aids also allows students with artistic ability to make distinctive contributions to the group. However, some groups which do not have such members often use photocopiers, especially the enlargement capabilities, to create adequate visuals. The first year I used this assignment, the entertainment reporter for one group put together a tape composed of segments from the best-selling songs of the year, which she played in the background while recounting the highlights of the year in music. Examining back issues of *Billboard* and using the record collection of a neighbor gave her all the material she needed.

Other groups have picked up this idea and used it in succeeding years. This past year, one entertainment reporter put together film clips from the best films of the year and played it while he covered the Academy Awards. Another group included commercials in its presentation, ensuring authenticity by using advertisements from old magazines. Groups for both 1990 and 1991 did a fashion review, with members of each group modeling costumes they found at home. Mentioning these types of creative variations from previous years usually stimulates new groups to come up with their own new ideas.

Each year, at least one group has surprised me with a new variation I haven't seen before.

I usually allocate three class periods for students to practice and polish their skits. Even though the final skits only need to be twenty minutes long, all of these class periods are necessary because students find that they have to make adjustments in their plans: what looks good in a written script does not always work well orally. Also, using visuals effectively or coordinating the use of tape recordings and videotape with the rest of their presentation requires multiple rehearsals so that it can be done smoothly and effectively. Each year the best groups have always done additional practice outside of class to achieve a good-quality product. At a minimum, allocating three days for practice sends the message to students that both what they do and how well they do it are important for this assignment.

The first year I used this assignment, I gave students two grades for the project, a group grade and an individual grade. Individual grades were based on research work and could be different for each member of the group. However, the collaborative nature of the assignment often made it difficult to determine who was responsible for a particular component of the final presentation, so now I give only group grades for the project. The group grade is based on the oral presentation plus research work and is the same for all members of the group. What do I consider in determining the grade? An examination of my evaluation sheet (figure 1) indicates what I consider important in making that determination. Students have to turn in their script, the notes they took while doing research (including photocopies), and a works cited page. These items allow me to evaluate the research component of the assignment.

If time allows, there are some worthwhile spin-off assignments that could be tied to these skits. For example, one year, when the game *Trivial Pursuit* was new on the market, groups created a 1970 *Trivial Pursuit* quiz that they administered to teachers and students from other classes. The low scores achieved by most respondents reinforced my students' belief that they had learned something while researching their projects. I have also had students write a persuasive composition concerning which event from their year seemed to be most significant and why they made the selection they did.

Three years of experience has made me an advocate for this assignment. I now look forward to viewing the presentations rather than dreading listening to the same rehashed speeches. No longer do I hear the proverbial question, "What if the speech isn't long enough?"

Evaluation of Group Presentations

TIME LIMIT (0–10 points)   ———
    Minus one point for each minute short of minimum
      requirement.

RESEARCH (0–10 points)   ———
    Amount of evidence that participants spent time gathering
      factual material.

PLANNING (0–10 points)   ———
    Was there a clear sense of organization?
    Did participants know what they were supposed to do and
      when?
    Any evidence of originality and/or uniqueness in the
      presentation?

DELIVERY (0–10 points)   ———
    Was there evidence that participants had rehearsed?
    Could all participants be heard clearly?
    Was there any "life" to the presentation—was it acted or
      simply read?

TOTAL POINTS   ———
GROUP GRADE   ———

Figure 1. Evaluation form for group presentations.

Even though the minimum requirement is a twenty-minute skit, typically, presentations run anywhere from twenty minutes to a full class period. I have also had the unique experience of having parents ask if they could visit the class when their son's or daughter's group gave its presentation—they have heard them talk so much about the project, or else their home was used for outside rehearsals. Finally, in their end-of-course evaluation, students almost always mention the project as the high point of the trimester. Writing about this assignment has made me start to wonder what creative variations my students will come up with this year. What more could teachers ask for than an assignment both they and their students enjoy?

Works Cited

Hoobler, Dorothy, and Thomas Hoobler. 1981. *An Album of the Seventies.* New York: Franklin Watts.

Leonard, Thomas, Cynthia Crippen, and Marc Aronson. 1988. *Day by Day: The Seventies*. 2 vols. New York: Facts on File Publications.

Urdang, Laurence, ed. 1981. *The Timetables of American History*. New York: Simon & Schuster.

V Learning in the Active Voice

We might agree that learning works best when it becomes an active process. We celebrate classrooms that involve the learners, that give them choices and respect their decisions, that put them to work with their learning tasks, that encourage linguistic, physical, and artistic manipulation of the concepts to be explored. Yet students report that in most of their classroom hours, they are seatbound, where they are expected to be passive receptacles—sponges or vessels, if you will—of instruction. The lecture-read-worksheet approach to instruction, these students suggest, has definite limitations and parameters.

In this section, we offer the experience of a wide range of teachers who share a common value for actively involving their students in learning tasks. They substantiate the sense of learning-as-activity, as, first of all, something to do.

In "Rx for an Anemic Classroom," Kathy Coffey reports in exciting detail about her colleague's kindergarten classroom where "learning is such joy that the eager [five-year-olds] practically beat down the classroom door" to get started. These students make choices from a range of exciting stimuli, become deeply engaged in learning, and experience self-esteem as they work with thematic materials and ideas.

Larry Johannessen, in "Taking the Flat Out of Teaching," prescribes a way to break the "frontal habit," that is, the teacher talking from the front of the room. He recommends having students test thematic generalizations in literature through vigorous, interactive discussion and debate, and in written, summative interpretation. The key to this approach is the application of a set of opinion statements to the students' own experiences and understanding of the literary selection.

In "Reporting a Metaphor," Susan Reese Brown demonstrates

the idea of an extended metaphor as an active means for students to express their feelings in safe, figurative terms.

Two essays report on classrooms that came alive when students picked their own books and talked with each other about them. Sarah Herz, in "Harmony and Excitement through Adolescent Literature," chronicles the change in her seventh-grade class when the students browsed independently through the fields of adolescent literature, recording their discoveries in response journals and persuading their classmates in book forums. Kathy Allen attracted reluctant readers to books by providing several copies each of young adult novels, then engaged the students in a teacher-guided "grand conversation" about the books. She details her experience in "Attracting Students to Reading."

In a confessional mode, Diann Gerke, in "Teacher's Loss, Students' Gain," reports how a lesson on point of view took on new and unexpected directions when students identified several other, more exciting possibilities with children's fairy tales.

In "From Donut Holes to Details," Dael Angelico-Hart enthusiastically shows how concrete objects can lead to a successful lesson in vocabulary that places value on individual effort, collaboration, and competition in ways that involve students at every turn.

In a reprise entitled "Thank You, Please," Susan Reese Brown gets her students going again on the commonplace matter of thank-you correspondence. When Aunt Matilda becomes involved, students become skillful, active practitioners of etiquette.

Rose Rosenthal was more than challenged by an assignment as a teacher of English as a second language, which she came to with no training, no program, and no materials. In "The Contemporary Challenge," she recounts how her independent development of a "total physical response" approach benefited both her second-language students and native speakers.

23 Rx for an Anemic Classroom

Kathy Coffey
Denver, Colorado

When Robert Fulgham proclaimed, "Everything I really needed to know I learned in kindergarten," he must have had a class like this in mind. The teacher, Janet Zander, cherishes children, builds their self-esteem, invites them to enjoy the drama and design, the power and play of language. Because she gives children a zest for learning language early in life, they are well prepared for the rest of the educational experience. Her classroom is a place for both teachers and parents to celebrate.

This kindergarten offers a feast for the senses: a blue bathtub with feet is crammed with pillows and books, a spot guaranteed to instill warm connotations for reading. The animals make soft snuffling noises; the children hum and chat quietly; the light glows in an incubator where "The Great Chicken Countdown" has begun. Easels abound; children's drawings and stories splash across every wall. The housekeeping area is transformed into a time machine this week; next week, it may become a covered wagon or a spaceship.

It is a rich environment for learning language—each week's activities focus on a different letter. For "F" week, firefighters visit; for "G" week, a goat takes up residence. During "H" week, a helicopter lands on the playground, and for "Q week," each child makes a quilt. How could anyone forget letters learned under delightful circumstances?

Underlying the bright aura is commitment to purposeful activity. Children are absorbed in work they have chosen themselves. At five different centers, they pursue math, alphabet, listening skills, story writing, and a choice of art, science or social studies. In one area, children close their eyes to listen to a poem so that they can "get a picture on their eyelids." At the bookshelf, young critics check for accuracy. (They have become critical readers since they discovered an error in a book. Megan's dark eyes flash as she corrects it: "Brachiosaurus didn't live in water!") Adam sings softly to himself as he colors; Mark and Sam discuss their projects.

None of the activity is random; everything relates to a central theme. If the unit focuses on the ocean, the children build a bathosphere from plastic sheets, paint ocean life on the "walls," inflate it with a fan, and climb aboard. If they are studying pioneers, they sing "My Darlin' Clementine" while drawing on fabric squares for their quilts. During dinosaur weeks, inflatable dinosaurs fill the chairs and hang from the ceiling; miniature dinosaurs, dinosaur eggs, dinosaur puppets, puzzles and graphs cover the tables. How does this relate to language? They design and write pop-up books about dinosaurs!

The advantage of the thematic approach is that it provides children with content for their writing. Just as college students can write trite papers about the prom or the football game, so too, the experience of a kindergartner can be thin material for stories. But children immersed in facts about space or oceans have a rich vocabulary and a wealth of facts to inform their stories. As they dictate, they use precise, sophisticated words correctly.

A faithful scribe, Mrs. Zander records the stories on small pieces of paper that fit onto the children's illustrations. When the paper was cut in the forms of clouds, Peter exalted, "I wrote a three-cloud story!" His parents were puzzled, until they had read it at least thirty times. They also enjoyed the ABC book he created with "hidden" letters. D's snuggle in the duck's bill; H's lurk in the roof of a house. Most important, Peter glows with pride as he points to his badge of ownership: "By Peter."

Asked about the pedagogy underlying her teaching, Mrs. Zander eschews educational jargon: "I just think it's best for the children. They learn so much: the names of all the planets from a song, 'Twinkle, Twinkle, Little Star' in Latin." She has tapped the energy of play; children learn as naturally as they breathe. A sage summed it up long ago: "Tell me, I forget. Show me, I remember. Involve me, I understand."

Perhaps the key to the children's involvement in their learning is the consistent way in which they are valued. Their choices count for so much that they spend the first twenty minutes each day on what *they* want to do. They choose what they need, even if they spend that time petting the duck. It gives the teacher a chance to catch up on everyone, and ask, "How are *you*, today?" Because this time is not a reward but a given, children line up for school expectantly, eager to begin. Seeing their excitement as they cluster at the door would make teachers of less zealous students envious.

The building of self-esteem carries over into class discussions, when Mrs. Zander goes to great lengths to turn a "wrong" answer into a teaching moment. "Maybe that wasn't quite what I was looking for," she will concede. "But let's talk about what you said." Perhaps the ultimate test of her creativity comes during the Friday session when children bring in objects starting with the letter they have focused on that week. One frazzled mother, confusing the show-and-tell list, consistently sent things starting with the wrong letter. Mrs. Zander rose to the challenge during "G" week, when Kevin proudly displayed a *Fire* engine. "Of course," she crowed, "it *Goes!*"

Much of her energy is poured into making children feel good about themselves, assuring them that no answer is wrong and that difference is a thing to celebrate. When one nonconformist folded all the paper lengthwise for a book he was writing, rather than in half, the more conventional way, he did not meet with disapproval: "Neat!" exclaimed Mrs. Zander. "You did it backwards!" That child took one step closer to being a risk taker and adventurer.

Difference is further celebrated with the international students who are members of the class. Other teachers might moan that nonnative speakers would consume more time and require more attention. Mrs. Zander treats them like kings and queens. Whenever the occasion arises, the children point out their native countries on maps or globes. For instance, "The dinosaurs migrated through Khairui's country, Malaysia, but they didn't get as far south as Citra's, Indonesia."

Native speakers learn many phrases from their honored guests: they can say "good morning" in Hebrew, German, Spanish, Japanese, and numerous other languages. They focus on how much they are *like* children in other countries, feeling sad, excited, or lonely in similar circumstances. Because their feelings are honored, they can more easily empathize with others. When they write a book about themselves for Mother's Day, it's entitled "Who in the World Am I?" Not the usual exercise in self-glorification, it places the child in an international context.

This global flavor carries into programs, in which children wear the costumes of other lands and sing holiday greetings in fifteen different languages. They taste the foods of other countries and learn their folk dances. A visitor from Kenya was surprised and pleased when the children greeted her in Swahili, counted to twenty in that language, and displayed their familiarity with the capital city and products of her native land.

Their global awareness enabled the students to write their own alphabet book about peace, with contributions such as: "C is for peace, because we want cats to keep crawling . . . J is for peace, because Jeremy, Jack, Joe, and Amber Jaries want peace . . . S is for peace, because peace is like a shooting star . . ." They were not even stumped by the letters that stall professional authors: "X is for peace because if we live in peace we won't become extinct . . . Z is for peace because zillions of people will survive."

Intensive learning occurs without resorting to worksheets, tests, or coercion. In the absence of pressure to learn language, children inhale it gladly. They move in a climate of praise, expressed simply in a touch, a compliment, a butterfly kiss. After they have sat motionless through a long story, they are rewarded: "Give yourselves a hand for listening so quietly!" After hearing, often enough, "You're such a good reader," or "That title makes me want to read on," a child fulfills a positive expectation.

In the Indian tradition, education begins with the students' questions; if they have none, the teaching process is irrelevant. Early in the launching stages of a unit, children are asked, "What do you want to learn? What do you think we'll find out?" They list their questions ("What size were dinosaur teeth? How big were their feet?"), avoiding the syndrome of a teacher dispensing information no one wanted or requested. Then the students set off on a process of discovery, probably as exciting to them as to researchers on the verge of historic breakthroughs. Different learning styles are stimulated in the hands-on environment: Sue may learn from music, Alex from rotating the diorama, Brian from reading.

Children are empowered by their choices and freed by the absence of misconceptions that everyone progresses at the same pace. Mrs. Zander laughs about her broad tolerance: "At the beginning of the year, one child's drawings looked like embryos. By the end, they looked like embryos with clothes on!"

Their theme for the year, "Children Can Make a Difference," found expression in many ways: they collected toys and coats for the poor at Christmas, and made a huge peace quilt which they raffled off. The proceeds bought an acre of rain forest, and helped offset hunger in the Sudan. What five-year-olds would not grow an inch or two in self-esteem, with a year of such credits to their names?

Their robust, rambunctious, self-directed pursuit of learning offsets the complaints often heard from educators at higher levels, where a common response to an assignment is, "How long does it hafta be?" Older students may seem bland and overly compliant because, somewhere along the way, they have lost the ownership of their learning process; they sit passively through discussions, rarely risking an opinion or challenging a theory. Self-esteem seems low among many such students, who write boring papers about subjects in which their investment is so minimal that they do not even bother to proofread or correct their mechanical and spelling errors.

Perhaps what they need is a return to the spirit of kindergarten, where egos are expansive and discussions heated, where a byline means that time and effort has been poured into a work, and where learning is such a joy that eager students practically beat down the classroom door to get in.

24 Taking the Flat Out of Teaching

Larry R. Johannessen
Saint Xavier University

In *A Place Called School*, John Goodlad (1984) describes the "flat" atmosphere in most classrooms, which is due to the dominance of the "frontal" teaching style—a style in which the teacher stands at the front of the class and talks, while the students listen, take notes, and repeat back what the teacher has said. This style, he says, has a dulling effect on young minds, killing their desire for learning and making school a lifeless experience. Goodlad recommends organizing classrooms to encourage more student inquiry, making them active seekers of knowledge rather than passive receptacles of facts. This focus on inquiry was also among the central recommendations of the English Coalition Conference that met in July 1987 to assess the teaching of English and to consider its future directions (Lloyd-Jones and Lunsford 1989; Elbow 1990). In response to the prescriptive recommendations of recent critics such as E. D. Hirsch (1987) and Diane Ravitch and Chester Finn (1987), coalition members, who came from diverse backgrounds and represented all levels of schooling, agreed to a platform calling for instruction that cultivates students' intellectual curiosity, rejecting the ideas that teaching involves imparting factual knowledge and that education is what Elbow (1990) describes as "list learning."

I have found that one effective way to break the traditional "frontal" teaching style habit is to incorporate opinionnaire activities into my teaching. What are opinionnaire activities and how do they work? The following excerpt from a class discussion of average, eleventh-grade high school students suggests much about the nature of these activities and how they work in the classroom.

> "That's not what the author is saying at all," Mary says. [She has interrupted Dan's rather long explanation of what he believed the author, John Collier, was trying to tell readers about love relationships, in his short story "The Chaser."]
> "Okay," Dan replies, "What do you think he means?"
> "Our group decided that the author would agree with

statement #13, 'Love never changes,' because Alan [the main character in the story] wants to buy the love potion and give it to Diane to make her love and sort of, like, worship him. He wants a love that never changes."

"Yes, Charles, you had your hand up," I interject.

"Our group saw this differently. Alan would agree that 'love never changes,' but not the author. That's the point of the story. That's why the old man who sells the potion to Alan says, at the end of the story, 'Au revoir.' Jenny, the French student in our group, told us that it means 'until we see each other again.' The old man knows that Alan will be back to buy the 'life-cleaner' or poison to kill Diane . . ."

"What? Come on!" a number of student voices chime in.

"Let me finish!" demands Charles. "See, the old man knows that after a while Alan will get sick of Diane adoring him—like the old man tells Alan, she will be 'jealous' and 'want to be everything to you.' See, the author wants us to realize that this isn't true love at all. Love does change."

"Oh, I get it!" Martha jumps in. "That's why he sells the love potion so cheap and the poison is so expensive. He knows Alan will get sick of this love and be back to buy the poison to get rid of Diane."

"Yeah, and now I get the title," Bill says. The word 'chaser' has two meanings here. It means someone who chases after someone or something, like Alan chases after Diane and what he thinks will be perfect love. But it also means a drink taken to wash down another drink, such as a drink of beer to wash down a shot of whiskey. So, like the poison is the beer or chaser to wash down the love potion or whiskey."

"He wants us to see that you can't force anyone to love you," Sharon adds. "It doesn't work. The author wouldn't agree with statement #13."

What the Discussion Reveals

How did this group of average, eleventh-grade high school students get to this rather sophisticated textual analysis of the short story? And why were they so involved in the discussion? And how could they have possibly understood the irony or ironies in the story without my lecturing to them first or telling them what irony is or at least what theme is?

The answer is at once simple and not so simple. First, despite what Hirsch and others might claim, I long ago gave up the notion that lecturing to students about irony, or having them read *the* definition of irony in their literature anthologies and then try to apply it to works of literature, would produce much real learning. Oh, sure, one or two students would "get it," but then they usually "got it" anyway. Real learning only happens when students become actively involved and can internalize knowledge or understanding by arriving at the realization themselves.

It is important to understand that the preceding excerpt from class discussion did not occur by accident. I began this sequence of instruction by first giving students fifteen generalizations about love, everything from "Love is blind" to "If you are really in love, physical appearance doesn't matter" (figure 1). I had them decide individually which generalizations they agreed with and which they did not. Then I compiled the results on the board, and we discussed the generalizations.

This discussion was heated and generated considerable disagreement. Of course, every teenager is interested in the subject of love, but the students were surprised to discover that class members held some very different views on the subject. With their enthusiasm ignited, I introduced the story. I suggested to them that authors who write love stories also have particular views about love, and they sometimes want to convince us that their views are right. "Let's read this story," I said, "and see if we can figure out what statements this author would agree or disagree with from our list of fifteen."

We read the story. Then the students got into small groups to answer the question I had posed. They didn't disappoint me. They enthusiastically debated various viewpoints. When they had arrived at agreement or when they could not agree in their small groups, we reconvened as a class.

The earlier excerpt illustrates the nature of the debate in class discussion: healthy, vigorous disagreement which took students, time and time again, back to the text for evidence to support their interpretations. In addition, a questioning audience encouraged students to explain carefully how their evidence supported their interpretations. I merely guided, directed, and made sure we moved forward toward a more complete understanding and comprehension of the text. I encouraged them to inquire, solve the problem, and synthesize.

Closure through Writing

After we discussed their understanding of the story, we then examined each of the fifteen generalizations about love and discovered that there was still disagreement about exactly which ones Collier would agree or disagree with and why.

Romantic Love/Marriage Opinionnaire

Directions: In the space provided, mark whether you agree or disagree with each statement.

Agree or Disagree

1. Teenagers cannot experience "true" love. _____
2. Love means never having to say you're sorry. _____
3. You can't expect a person to change his or her habits after marriage. _____
4. It is better to have loved and lost than never to have loved at all. _____
5. No one is ever too young to fall in love. _____
6. Love is blind. _____
7. You have to work at love. _____
8. Physical attraction must precede true love. _____
9. Love at first sight is possible. _____
10. If you're really in love, physical appearance doesn't matter. _____
11. In love relationships, "opposites attract." _____
12. If someone does not return your affection, the best thing to do is to keep trying to change his or her mind. _____
13. Love never changes. _____
14. For the most part, being in love is "a pain in the neck." _____
15. If you truly love someone, you will not be attracted to anyone else. _____

Figure 1. Romantic love/marriage opinionnaire. (Adapted from Kahn, Walter, and Johannessen 1984, 35–38; Johannessen 1989, 40–43. Used with permission.)

"Tomorrow," I said to them, "I am going to ask you to write an essay explaining why you think Collier would agree or disagree with the statements we are having problems with here. Write it as a letter to one of the people in the class who disagrees with you. Try to convince this person that he or she is wrong. Yes, Steve, do you have a question?"

"Can we use things from the story to prove our point? You know, like Charles did when we discussed?"

"Can you? That's exactly what I want you to do."

"Can we start it tonight if we want?" Darlene asked.

"Sure!" I said.

The bell rang and I knew that some of the enthusiasm would be gone when they came to class the next day. One or two would forget their stories, and another one or two would forget their list of generalizations about love. I would also need to review the end of our discussion, as well as the assignment. I would have to cajole one or two to get busy and stop talking, but I knew that some of the momentum would still be there.

Even though the new problem of writing their interpretations would present new anxieties and a new struggle for both them and me, I knew that real learning was going on. I knew, too, that we could fall back on what we learned *today* as a reminder that they could do it. And I knew they would feel additional anxiety as well as a sense of struggle when we begin working on Max Shulman's story, "Love Is a Fallacy," two days from now, but I also knew that they were already halfway there.

I have used this opinionnaire with a number of literary works that involve the theme of romantic love/marriage, including Shakespeare's *Romeo and Juliet*. I have found it and the follow-up activities described here an effective approach for getting students interested in the ideas they will encounter in particular literary works. I have also found it an effective approach for helping them to link their own views to the literature as well as to think and write critically about it. Using activities like these in our teaching can invigorate literary study, help students become more independent learners, and improve the ambiance in our classrooms.

Works Cited

Elbow, Peter. 1990. *What Is English?* New York: MLA and NCTE.

Goodlad, John. 1984 *A Place Called School: Prospects for the Future.* New York: McGraw.

Hirsch, E. D., Jr. 1987. *Cultural Literacy: What Every American Needs to Know.* Boston: Houghton.

Johannessen, Larry R. 1989. "The Nature of Love: Two Short Stories." In *The Best of NOTES Plus: Practical Classroom Activities for Junior and Senior High School Students*, edited by Ruth K.J. Kline, 40–43. Urbana: NCTE.

Kahn, Elizabeth A., Carolyn Calhoun Walter, and Larry R. Johannessen. 1984. *Writing about Literature.* Urbana: ERIC and NCTE.

Lloyd-Jones, Richard, and Andrea A. Lunsford, eds. 1989. *The English Coalition Conference: Democracy through Language.* Urbana: NCTE and MLA.

Ravitch, Diane, and Chester E. Finn. 1987. *What Do Our 17-Year-Olds Know? A Report on the First National Assessment of History and Literature.* New York: Harper.

25 Reporting a Metaphor

Susan Reese Brown
Durango High School, Durango, Colorado

Do you ever long to know how your students are feeling as people, deep down in their hearts? Do you wish they would communicate with you in a sincere, simple, honest way? In the swift, swirling rush of day-to-day classroom activities and wall-to-wall students, who among us has the luxury of this kind of communication? Even if students were bold enough to risk open, oral communication, would there be time enough, opportunity enough, for each voice to be heard? Perhaps, but probably not.

The dew-fresh countenance, the furrowed brow, the red and glazed eyes, the vibrant glow, the limpid pallor are there in the kaleidoscope of student faces familiar to any teacher. But how to read the stories on the faces and hear the songs in their hearts has always been a challenge for me. One early morning, as I was hoping to truly connect with my students as fellow human beings—all 150 of them—the idea of a metaphor report came to me. I tried it in each of my six freshman English classes that day. It worked. It had power. It had scent. It exhibited potential for sheer poetry, as well as for teaching students figurative language and thinking.

The metaphor reporting activity I created works something like this:

First, I share an up-to-the-minute, sincere, extended metaphor of my own which expresses how I am feeling. The metaphor might be something like this:

> I am a gardener working hard to till, plant, water, fertilize, and weed. I am excited about the flowers and fruit my garden will bear. I eagerly seek signs of new growth on each plant and enjoy the development of the plants. Many plants flourish. Some don't though. I wonder why. Could I do more? Should I do less for their care? Why won't they blossom?

Students might interpret my metaphor, for instance, by saying that the gardening efforts are my teaching efforts, that the growth of the plants represents their progress as students, and that I wonder why some students are not working and producing. Should students leave out segments of the metaphor in their interpretation, I prod gently with leading questions. Here, for example, I might ask what my weeding represents.

Students are then invited to reflect on how they are, what they are feeling, what the status of their being is and to select an appropriate metaphor for communicating their perceptions. I am careful not to put images into their heads by providing too many examples. Usually, three or four examples will suffice. I might ask if they are feeling like a car in need of an overhaul, a brand-new car eager for the road, a broken-down car? A short-order or gourmet cook? A millionaire or a pauper?

Students then write without interruption for ten to fifteen minutes. They are encouraged to keep writing even if they think they have fully expressed their metaphor. The silence rule is strictly maintained. When they are finished, they hand in their papers, having already been told they will not get personal, written responses from me, but rather a silent, mental response of quiet and respectful reading. On a subsequent day, and with the permission of the writers, I read aloud the metaphors that touched me the most. Students participate in interpreting peer metaphors respectfully and empathetically.

The range of symbols presented by the students is impressive and as richly diverse as both their backgrounds and life itself. For example, "I am" is connected with metaphors such as being on a bucking bronco, in a whirlwind, in a runaway semi truck going nowhere in a hurry, the sun, a free soaring eagle, a turtle, at the base of a cliff, on a tiny life raft in the middle of the ocean, the leaves on a tree, in quicksand, in a fun house filled with mirrors.

The messages of the word pictures are very often drawn with such intense clarity that invaluable insights into individuals and their current challenges are brought into focus, definitely for me, and I trust for the students themselves. For example, my perception of my eighth-hour class clown adjusted significantly after reading his metaphor:

> I am an old couch. People just come along, use me for comfort and enjoyment, then leave and forget about me. I work hard at my job in life to make other peoples' lives better. I make people laugh and they like it. But after awhile they leave me, forget the laughter and how I work to make them happy and move on.

Likewise, how could I help but perceive differently an underachieving, gifted student after reading his metaphor:

> I am in a trash dumpster sifting through banana peels, cardboard boxes, wet papers, aluminum cans, and baby diapers. I am

looking for a treasure. Though I do not think I will find one, I dig through the rubbish farther.

Then, from the look-alike teenage girl comes this touching cry for uniqueness:

I am a single dandelion in a field of hundreds trying so hard to stand out and be different, but it seems the more I try, the harder it is and the more I fail.

At times these pictures are piercingly poetic:

I sit in a garden. It's a beautiful garden with bright flowers and a crystal waterfall. I'm feeling happy, but I turn the brightness of the garden over to find the tarnish. How long will the garden last before the cold winter kills it?

In rarer instances, the metaphors evoke virgin poetry:

I am Romeo.
I find the one I cannot know.
I fall in love, but it's a fact
That fate's cruel hand
Twists the knife in my back.
I've played the fool for everyone
And cried until the morning sun
Showed its rays in the dawn.
And then I dried up every tear,
Went to school and sat so near
To the one I loved.
It's sad, but true
That my love is all for you.
But will I ever touch your face
Or take you to that special place
Where we could sit each summer day
And push the mean cruel world away?

Since that first day of trying out the metaphor report, I have put it to work numerous times, always to good effect. Through it I can talk heart to heart with my students and have them speak back. Metaphor reporting has the further advantage, however, of fostering poetic and figurative thinking, which enriches students' writing and their interpretation of literature. Students are therefore much better equipped to build in figurative language in their own writings. How easy it becomes to bridge to the interpretation of characters in stories, novels, and drama with the question, "What is his metaphor report?" Likewise, students' rehearsals in being metaphors themselves definitely help them recognize symbols and symbolic thinking in all genres.

As facile as this activity may appear, I know it offers much to my students and me. At a minimum, it enables me to hear as honest a reply as the students are willing to offer to the sincere question, "How are you?" As their teacher, I am helped greatly, for I really want to know.

26 Harmony and Excitement through Adolescent Literature

Sarah K. Herz
Coleytown Middle School, Westport, Connecticut

It was not a good situation; I was traveling between the senior high and a middle school, and my seventh graders were sending me over the edge. That September I found a set of short stories in the seventh-grade book room; we read and discussed them without much enthusiasm. Then I tried *Shadow of a Bull* by Maia Wojciechowska, which did not ignite a big spark, either. The students were not pleased at all, and by the time I handed out *Lilies of the Field* by William Barrett, our classroom environment was quite unpleasant. We had our good days and bad days, but I would characterize most of them as bad.

They moaned and groaned about *Lilies of the Field*; they criticized it constantly. Somehow we slogged through it, and I showed the movie and asked them to write a comparison of the book and the film. They liked the movie, and their writing indicated that they really had some valid opinions about what they disliked in the novel. Their writing was clear and well organized. But our classroom environment still needed a boost.

After a period of heated discussion, the students convinced me that they wanted to read books that were more interesting and more exciting. They persuaded me that they wanted to select their own titles. How? By using the school library and listing recent books they had read which they really enjoyed. Since they seemed confident and honest about the kinds of books they wanted to read, I agreed to let them choose their own titles. They brought in books from home, and we visited our school library. I also brought in some titles from the book room—so they had several possibilities. We agreed that they would finish their books within two weeks. I developed the following list of reading-response questions:

Describe how you felt after reading this story.

Which part of the story made you happy? Sad? Angry? Explain your feelings.

Which character in the story did you want to protect?

What questions would you like to ask the main character?

Did the author write a believable story? Explain.

At what point in the story does the main character make an important decision?

There were at least twenty questions to choose from. They taped the response questions inside the front covers of their response journals and used them in writing their journal entries. We agreed that every other Friday we would have a book forum where students would "booktalk" the books they felt that other classmates would enjoy. When more than one student read the same title, those students would form a panel and present the book to the class.

We set aside two of our six weekly language arts periods to read, write, and conference about our reading books. Most students were finishing their books quickly, so some were in the library selecting new titles, some were writing or having a conference with me, and some were reading or, if they had read the same title, might be discussing a title in pairs out in the hall. Sometimes we would spend a class period listing titles on the board. Then we talked about the criteria they were using in their response writing about these novels. As the recorder at the board, I listed comments as we went around the class.

And guess what? They were discussing plot, suspense, surprise, character, main idea, author's purpose, and all the good stuff that we English teachers think we have to point out each year in our lessons on the elements of literature. It was remarkable to discover that these students could be independent readers and learners, that they could shape meaning from the books they read, that they could discuss books with enthusiasm, with curiosity, and with critical opinions backed up by facts and interpretation.

The writing responses in their journals were full of insight, too. Here is a quote from a previously passive nonreader, who was usually unprepared and bored in class, writing about Williams Sleator's *Inter-stellar Pig*: "I exploded after I was done with the novel . . . it was so full of suspicion throughout the beginning and when the end came, it was very startling." As the semester went on, he read constantly and came into the room ready to discuss his titles and exchange ideas with other students. He was alive and reading, and enjoying reading, because he chose his own books.

A complainer, who had once told me she had no time to read, wrote about Amy Ehrlich's *Where It Stops Nobody Knows:* "I had many predictions throughout the book, and the fact that Joyce wasn't her real mother is what I least expected. . . . I'm really glad I read this book, because I've learned a lot about relationships from it. This book has a strong plot." There were so many signals of the critical, sustained reading that was in process in our classroom.

Another passive, quiet, well-behaved student wrote about Steven Levenkron's *The Best Little Girl in the World:* "There are some terrible problems we have to face in our life, and if we try our hardest we can get rid of them . . . It's important to learn about anorexics and their problems." Because she enjoyed this novel so much, she read the sequel, *Kessa:* "After reading the first four chapters, I didn't really like it because it was just flashbacks from his previous novel, but I continued reading and there were many, many new problems." How many teachers have tried to force students to continue reading when they've complained about the opening chapters of a novel?

The importance of the reading-response journals cannot be stressed enough—the personal responses in these journals were reflective and meaningful. They were interesting and exciting for me to read, so I looked forward to a private dialogue with each student in my response to their writing—a far cry from "grading papers" that are on the same topic and become monotonous. I was reading about books—all kinds of characters and situations. I looked forward to reading their response journals, and I read them with pleasure. They were not graded until the students selected a particular response that they would develop into a piece of writing.

I listened during book forums, and I, too, was a participant. As I read many of these adolescent novels, I began to understand students' enthusiasm and pride in their reading. Adolescent novels are accessible: there is a wide range of reading levels, the main character is an adolescent, and the stories are about situations and topics which are real to teenagers. And like adult literature, there is a variety of genres— romance, fantasy, science fiction, adventure, history, humor, mystery, and more.

The classroom environment changed in many ways. We enjoyed one another's comments more and more; our discussions began to focus on books that had similar or different characters facing the same circumstances. Students initiated discussion about action/plot, dialogue, description. They gently argued about whether or not characters would behave in the manner they exhibited in the novels. They criticized the author for "fakery," what we English teachers might refer to as "contrivance." They had taken command of their reading, and through their reading-response journals, they reflected on their reading and used their written reflections as a basis for discussion.

I think this whole experience was a strong lesson for me. I had lost touch with young adult or adolescent literature. Oh, I had read and taught *The Chocolate War* by Robert Cormier; I had read Hinton's *The Outsiders; That Was Then, This Is Now;* and *Rumblefish;* and I, too, had been touched by *Go Ask Alice.* But I had not revisited adolescent literature for many years. I now found it fresh, vibrant, and exciting; I was moved by some wonderful authors, especially Ouida Sebestyen, Virginia Hamilton, Walter Dean Meyers, and Sue Ellen Bridgers. What excellent writers!

I came to realize that students could enjoy discussing literature as much as talking about sports, social life, television, or themselves. When they said, "Ms. Herz, you've got to read this book," I felt included, and what a wonderful feeling that was. By the time we were scheduled to read Shakespeare's *A Midsummer Night's Dream,* I brought in the books and they took over. We cast the parts every day or so and read the entire play aloud. Everyone participated. When some parts or characters were confusing, a couple of mavens politely explained what was going on. They organized skits and enjoyed themselves, and so did I.

I remember a student who read Betty Green's *Summer of My German Soldier* and wrote:

> I did not think I would be able to continue it because the first four chapters are extremely boring. But in the middle you start to understand the characters and grieve for their problems. After finishing, you cry. Patty risked her family's pride for a love no one could compare to.

And because this student wanted to understand more about the Nazis, she read Barbara Ragosky's *Smoke and Ashes* and shared her feelings:

> I feel I have a new understanding of the Holocaust . . . It is astonishing to see how our world could let such a horrible thing happen. One of the things that surprised me the most in this book was the will to stay alive . . . people struggled through starvation and mental and physical cruelty without giving up. Their passion for life touched me.

And so my students' passion about what they were reading

touched me. They convinced me that they are the best judges of what they enjoy and understand in literature. And, as they gained confidence in discussing and critiquing what they read, they were more open and more comfortable with the required curriculum. I am grateful to them for introducing me to a whole world of literature I had ignored—the world of adolescent literature. Their honesty and enjoyment of that literature led me to a year-long sabbatical—studying, researching, and reading adolescent literature and sharing current adolescent literature with other students and teachers in our school system.

And maybe next time we'll try reading *Lilies of the Field* in May.

27 Attracting Students to Reading

Kathy Allen
Palos Verdes Intermediate School,
Palos Verdes Estates, California

Throughout my professional career, I have always focused on reluctant readers—typically boys who are vocal about their dislike of reading. When I was assigned to the intermediate grades, I found myself teaching a whole class of seventh and eighth graders who made it obvious that they had never enjoyed reading a book. Their backgrounds were similar, having spent years in elementary schools filling in thousands of blanks on worksheets.

Once, I naively asked my students why they elected to take my class when they felt so negatively about reading. A boy answered: "You mean I had a choice?" That was when I learned the distinction between regular electives and "required" electives. Realizing that the students and I were in this thing together, I undertook two giant tasks: (1) reading enough young adult fiction to select books that would engage my readers; and (2) organizing the class so that all students would succeed with the minimum requirements of reading and responding to quality pieces of literature.

The small successes I experienced with these reading skills classes led me to a deeper question: How do I develop a love of reading in my students that will lead to a lifelong reading habit? Are my students ready to take their places in a nation of readers, or are they going to become nonreading adults? I refuse to believe that any of my students are lost to the wonder of fiction at the ripe, old ages of twelve and thirteen. If I could find a way to get them to read on their own and then provide them with an opportunity to talk with others who had read the same book, would they get "hooked"?

Two serendipitous encounters provided the impetus for me. First, in reading current research, I came across a term, "grand conversations," coined from a remark made by Jim Higgins, when he was at the University of Arizona. I love what the term "grand conversations" implies. Second, listening to a presentation by Carole

Urzúa, I heard her plea for second language learners: "Our children should read silently, everyday, from books they choose" and "have a payoff for reading and constructing meaning, such as sharing a favorite part of a story with a friend." Now here was a person who shared my own conviction about students and reading for fun.

Enthusiastically, I approached my new semester with a bonus option: read any book from my book box, I told them, and discuss it with a small group after the reading. I explained that I planned to tape their conversations for a research project I was doing at UCLA on youths and reading. Each week I religiously marked down the progress of their extended reading and listened to varied excuses as to why they had not read. The situation became quite desperate, and I envisioned the term's end arriving with no book discussions having taken place. Then, in the last weeks of the semester, precipitated by interim reports going home, the students began to jump into action. They began to schedule taping sessions, and I actually taped two groups who had completed *Be a Perfect Person in Just Three Days* and one group which had read *Dollhouse Murders*.

As I hovered excitedly nearby, it dawned on me that the taping was not going to be as easy as I had anticipated. That first taping was going to be nothing but background noise unless I stepped in with some questions to stimulate their talk—I learned that students are not used to talking without teacher direction. It was impossible to get them started and hard to keep the conversation going, but they got better at it, and so did I. I now give them a set of questions, based on Judith Langer's (1990) research, the day before the taping session so that they can make notes. And I let friends be in the same session.

In scripting the tapes of these book discussions, I discovered several things. Students participated freely in wonderful conversations about the books they had read. Also, the context of the conversations demonstrated literal comprehension, statements clarifying understanding, supportive and evaluative statements as well. Often students would relate to the main character and evaluate his or her actions based on what they themselves would do under the same circumstances. Some even critiqued the writing ability of an author. My students reacted positively to the book discussions and took the whole situation quite seriously.

One semester and four taping sessions, however, do not qualify as a definitive study, but it encouraged me to continue the bonus book groups in my reading skills classes. I hope this paper encourages you to try book groups, especially with students who are reluctant to pick up a book and read. To get you started, I offer the following six suggestions:

1. Select only five or six titles—real grabbers. Have four or five copies of each in the book group box.

2. Present or talk about each of the titles with the class.

3. Self-selection is very important. (I usually keep one or two extra copies in case of disappointment!)

4. Allow some silent reading time in class and also encourage fifteen to twenty minutes of reading at home. My students can earn bonus points for reading at home and getting their timecards signed.

5. Each week, record the number of pages read. The students may need encouragement at first. I also have a rule: you must read fifty pages before trading in a book.

6. Schedule book discussions as soon as four students complete a given book. Allow everyone in the book group to participate in the discussion, even if someone is not finished.

The questions for discussion need to be general, not detail-specific. Students do not want to list the characters or sequence of events when they finish reading; they want to find out what others thought about the book in order to get a deeper understanding or a special insight. The role of the teacher requires that you lead the discussion by asking questions which stimulate talk among the students. If an opportunity arises to teach a literary form or to provide background information, by all means, do so. But remember, book groups provide the students with a rare opportunity to collaborate. Everyone's interpretation is valid.

In order for book groups to be successful, the teacher must model the role of a reader; therefore, I read the books that I present to the class. My students would know immediately if I did not like a book, so I choose only my favorites. I look forward to the discussions of the books and can hardly wait until the students have finished reading so we can talk.

Work Cited

Langer, Judith. 1990. "Understanding Literature." *Language Arts* 67: 812–16.

28 Teacher's Loss, Students' Gain

Diann Gerke
Waite High School, Toledo, Ohio

My experience as a teacher has taught me at least one truth: I am never truly in control of a lesson, not even in its formulation. I had planned a simple, two-class-period lesson to illustrate point of view and its vital role in storytelling. Using Jon Scieszka's *The True Story of the Three Little Pigs*, which tells the incident from the wolf's vantage point, I had intended that the students compare the two stories, the parody and the original, noting that, with the change of viewpoint, the outcome was likewise changed. This springboard was to result in a writing assignment in which my students were to rewrite a fairy tale or nursery rhyme from another point of view.

The theoretical basis for this lesson came from research I had done on creativity in students. One aspect of creativity, according to J. P. Guilford, in his conceptual model of creativity, is adaptive flexibility, which requires skills used in a familiar medium to be modified and integrated into a different but related one (Guilford 1959, 147–48). Therefore, with the example from Scieszka's book, the viewpoint of the wolf was to be examined for its similarities and differences to the original, concerning specifically what really happened in each of the wolf's meetings with the three pigs, what resulted from those encounters, and what the wolf's ultimate reputation became. The students were then to choose a piece, examine its point of view, noting specifically the influence that point of view had on the character's actions and the plot of the story. Following this phase, they were to select an opposing point of view and determine what changes in plot and characterization would have to be made as a result.

At this point, control of the lesson and my planning ended. Rather than focusing on the flexible nature of point of view, my students began asking, "Can we illustrate our stories? Hey, how about letting us read these to the class? No, wait, can we read these to little kids?" My lesson plan was instantly reformulated. Soon we were enmeshed in plans for visits to elementary schools. The students became so enthusiastic that they were pleading with their other teachers to cover my classes so we could be gone. They also decided to send a list of the parodied stories to the teachers of the classes we would visit to ensure the elementary students' familiarity with the original stories. I also lost out on my plan to use the revision groups in the later stages of the process. (My aim that year had been to establish effective group work at all stages of writing.) Instead, my authors became quite secretive and refused to let anyone from the class get a preview of their work.

I may have lost control of the lesson plans, but what the students gained from empowering themselves made that loss negligible by comparison. Their results were phenomenal. Titles such as "Little Miss(fit) Muffet," "Three Billie Goats Tough," and "The Little Merman" highlighted wonderful stories of adventure, imaginatively illustrated, garnered from favorite childhood memories.

An unplanned but rewarding lesson came from one particular student named Shawn. He had been in the class for six weeks, feeling thoroughly intimidated and resentful because my honors class had been forced upon him. Shawn was convinced he was a misfit and could make no contribution to the class, and he manifested his resentment daily. His attitude, however, fell by the wayside as quickly as had my lesson plans. Shawn had deliberately chosen for his parody a selection that he knew I would disapprove of on grounds of racial stereotyping. Despite my objections, he went ahead with his plan, but surprisingly, he changed the thrust of the tale to avoid racial stereotyping and to present traditionally maligned characters in a new and favorable light. Nonetheless, our visits to elementary students were only of incidental interest to Shawn. His real triumph came in the reaction of his classmates to the reading of his story. Through his insightful story and marvelous caricatured illustrations, Shawn had demonstrated his writing voice, which demanded his peers' attention and regard. From that day forward, the class was still challenging but never again impossible for Shawn.

I was later informed that my class was not the only beneficiary of our works. My students' enthusiasm and creativity infected other classrooms. The elementary students, in fact, wanted to try their hands at rewriting stories. Later on, their teachers sent their work to us for our enjoyment.

A second truth I have drawn from this experience is that whenever a lesson gets out of control, I let it. I sit back and watch my students determine some of their own curriculum, and we all reap the benefits.

Work Cited

Guilford, J. P. 1959. "Traits of Creativity." In *Creativity and Its Cultivation,* edited by H. M. Anderson, 142–61. New York: Harper & Row.

29 From Donut Holes to Details

Dael Angelico-Hart
Dunn Middle School, Danvers, Massachusetts

During my long commute to work, I thought about how much I needed a lesson—something to get the attention of a difficult class of fifth graders, so I immediately thought of concrete, hands-on objects. But it was 7:00 a.m., I was on a major thoroughfare, and as always, I had little time to spare. I stopped for the sure-fire motivator, food, and bought two dozen donut holes, enough for me to use to divide up my class evenly into teams of six. By adding the element of competition to a concrete, edible object, I was on my way to an exceptional lesson.

So, start with objects, ones with a distinguishing characteristic that can naturally divide up your class into teams of four to six members each. Donut holes, in a limited variety of flavors, have always been extremely successful. But I have also used my five-year-old son's Duplo blocks, which naturally fall into four color categories. A colleague of mine used valentine heart candies, which also had a similar color attribute. But in a pinch, I have used paper clips, rubber bands, thumbtacks, and erasers. The beginning is a concrete object on the desk, in front of each student. There is absolutely no substitute for the real thing staring each competitor in the eye.

Next, pass out a piece of paper to each student. Then, ask your students to observe their object, since they will be given three minutes to write as many single words about it as possible; you may add the terms "describing word" or "adjective" or simply leave it as "words about the object," depending on the age of the children involved. Have them begin as you would with any standardized test, to emphasize the seriousness of the task at hand, and then let them write. If I am using donut holes, for example, I stop after three minutes, give them a chance to slowly enjoy their treat, and then give them another minute to add some newly acquired words. (Blueberry or cherry holes offer some new possibilities after they are tasted.)

Now divide the students into teams according to some attribute of the object—the donut holes by flavor, blocks or candies by color. The teams should be random but multi-ability grouped.

Once in teams, each group should appoint a secretary, maybe by picking the student with the longest initial list of words. The secretary then reads his or her list while the other members of the team check off any duplicate words on their respective lists. Each team member then repeats this procedure, reading only new words that have not yet been read. The secretary records all new words and thus compiles a master list for the team. The last person to read will obviously have the least number of words to read, so it should be mentioned to the class beforehand that this is not a reflection on the individual, but a natural result of the process.

Each team then sends its secretary up to the front of the room with a master team list. The same process is then repeated to compile a master list for the class. However, a competitive element is added. A single point is given for each word on the team's list, while two points are given for each word that is unique to that list. As in all contests, the decision of the judge, whether it be a student or students or the teacher, is final. With older students, it is best to set the ground rules ahead of time: for example, "We are only looking for adjectives" or "We will resolve any arguments with the dictionary." I, however, like to accept creative words that follow grammatical rules, such as "blueberryish," but the important point is to simply lay out some guidelines, since the competition does tend to become keen. And be sure to keep track of the scores as each team reads its list.

This classroom activity is time-consuming, the whole lesson requiring almost an hour, but the rewards are worth it. The immediate end result is a classroom full of excited children who have stretched themselves to the limit of their own vocabulary as well as listened and shared in the vocabulary of others. My students, for instance, have begun to use specific words and have gone beyond vocabulary such as "nice" and "beautiful." There is also a long list of student-generated vocabulary that can be utilized as spelling or vocabulary lists or within themes or stories. And all for the reward of an extra donut hole to the winning team!

When the winning team has been declared, this is a good time to ask, "Did anyone describe the donut hole as 'quiet' or 'curious'?" Depending on the quality of their answers, give them these or other examples that slightly exceed the limits of the vocabulary they have used. Focus on all the senses, even with the paper clips and thumbtacks: "Did anyone describe their thumbtack as 'tasteless'?" Unique responses have been rewarded in a new way, in a way more lasting than a comment on a theme such as "Use better descriptive words!" ever could.

If this lesson is motivational and extends vocabulary the first time around, its effect is stronger on the second go-round. A week or so later, try the same lesson with a different object and see the specific descriptors the students use when they know the competition is on.

Why does this lesson work so well? First, it is automatically individualized within a heterogeneous group: each student has the same time limit. Some students will spell six words incorrectly while some will write thirty-six words perfectly. The slowest and the fastest students are working side by side, at their own pace, on the same task—each will have something to contribute to the class. If you anticipate that some of the slower students might have their entire list eliminated within their group before it is their turn to read, you can appoint the person with the *least* number of words as secretary.

Second, the lesson automatically lends itself to cooperative learning. The random selection of donut holes, Duplo blocks, or paper clips generates the multi-ability, cooperative learning groups. Each student in the group participates. All students have something valid to contribute.

Third, the lesson encourages what Madeleine Hunter calls "active participation; participation by all of the students, all of the time." No one is sitting daydreaming while someone else is doing the work. Every student is engaged, writing, and contributing. And when the time comes to compile a master list for the team, every student must listen in order to make the process work.

Fourth, the lesson uses many of the practices of the whole language philosophy. It uses words from the students' own experiences, and it has a strong oral and written component. Just as in the "big books," the same words are repeated in either written or oral form no fewer than five times during this lesson. And they are student-generated words, not those of a textbook. If the word lists are then used again in a story (a natural is "My Life Story as a Donut Hole"), the whole language circle is complete.

Try it. You won't just like it—you'll love it.

30 Thank You, Please

Susan Reese Brown
Durango High School, Durango, Colorado

Call me a fuddy-duddy. Call it my pet peeve. Call it nostalgia for Emily Post. Whatever you might say, I decry the decline in the art of thank-you notes. Worst of all, I decry those who do not even acknowledge receipt of a gift through a written thank-you note. But almost as bad is the bland note which reads, "Thank you for the present. Love, Lufa Lou," or the blatantly error-ridden note which lacks even the conventions of proper form. Because these inadequacies bother me so much, I have undertaken a personal crusade to instruct every student who enters my high school English classes in the art of writing a proper thank-you note. Student arguments that attempt to convince me that particular individuals are somehow exempt from the need to know this point of etiquette fall on deaf ears. Besides, I have Aunt Matilda on my side.

Prior to calling in Aunt Matilda, I have attempted to make the case for writing thank-yous through the following steps. First, right after Christmas vacation, I play devil's advocate, with the lead, "Why write thank-you notes, anyway? You already have the presents." After being set straight by those valiant students who urge the courtesy, I continue to press my case about not ever having received a single word about the many gifts I have given in the past. Then, I proceed to read personal examples of banal thank-you notes that acquaintances have received and to follow up with exemplary notes. Next, the class tries to determine what makes the good examples good. At this point, I detail ingredients of a sound thank-you note, giving each student an individual checklist that includes the following points:

1. Give the present its exact name and a sound description.
2. Indicate how you will use and enjoy it.
3. Refer to the time, energy, and sentiment involved in the giving of the gift.
4. Include personal and/or family news, if appropriate.
5. Use a friendly letter form.
6. Edit carefully for accuracy.

By now, students know for sure what's coming. Indeed, they are to practice an ideal thank you—either for a holiday present they have not yet acknowledged or one they wish they had gotten but didn't. These are peer-edited and then submitted to me for a critique. Each form infraction, omission of content, and grammatical error is noted. These notes are returned to the students, and then the class reviews the problem areas. After that, the fun begins. Aunt Matilda's long and eagerly awaited gifts arrive.

For her gifts, I use the world of mail order catalogs for my shopping mall. I use picture ads of the most peculiar and humorous gifts imaginable and tape them onto colored stationery. Their arrival is no minor occasion, for Aunt Matilda is beloved, ancient, childless, and filthy rich. Furthermore, everyone knows she has a particular fondness for her teenage nieces and nephews. Coupled with her zeal for giving what she regards as exactly the perfect gift is her penchant for propriety. Any thank-you note that reaches her hands needs to be flawless.

For the students, a successful thank-you note is no problem—they are motivated, on many levels, to write their best. After dispensing the treasures at random, I allow time for students to compare and barter gifts; the one each settles on will be the object of the note. This creates further interest and excitement. Aunt Matilda is to be thanked effusively for sweatshirts with iridescently radiating stellar constellations, furry dog and cat slippers, rockin' chicken alarm clocks, ladybug and bumblebee puppets, Monopoly watches, ballerina penguin teapots and mugs, and kitchen and household items no one even knew existed. The resulting official thank-you notes are humorous and enjoyable. They test the students' descriptive powers and allow them a full range of hyperbolic tendencies. Grades for these second efforts are entered in the grade book.

Consider the following note written by a freshman student for a soap and shampoo rack designed to span the width of a bathtub—admittedly just the gift every red-blooded, fifteen-year-old would cherish:

Jan. 5, 1991

Dear Aunt Matilda,

Happy New Year! How was your Christmas? Mine was pretty bad until I received your gift. The sink shelf/storage basket/food rack is one of the best gifts anyone has ever given to me. The pearl white coating is smooth as a baby's rear and very easy to clean. The design is sophisticated and technologically superior to other brands. The rack, the most durable I have ever seen, has held up under heavy use. Suspension bridges should be made as well. My roommate, the world's greatest cook, wants to trade her new Macintosh computer for it. It would not be a fair trade; my rack is better. I use it for everything. Thank you for this dynamite gift!

Love,

Shane

Aunt Matilda has never failed me or my students. Her fictitious reality, appealing so readily to the imagination of us all, makes the task of teaching and learning the writing of thank-you notes as exciting as unwrapping the present in the first place. Well, almost. Regardless, I trust that students have acquired the skill of writing an adequate thank-you note and will be motivated to use this skill in the future.

31 The Contemporary Challenge

Rose Rosenthal
Morningside High School, Inglewood, California

Many language arts teachers are faced with the challenge of teaching English to students who speak little or no English. Few English teachers have had any training in teaching these students, and many of us have no materials to help us. Two years ago, "Beginning English as a Second Language" appeared on my teaching schedule with no advance notice. In all my twenty years of teaching, I had taught English to students who spoke the language. Suddenly, I was faced with a class of youngsters who stared at me blankly when I asked, "How are you?" Having no training and no materials, I had to develop my own methods from the start. I scratched my head plenty!

Finally, I began jumping around, pointing to things, putting signs on everything, bringing in bottles labeled "poison," clearing my pantry and refrigerator at home to find items to show my class. Now, I know that I was using an approach known as Total Physical Response (TPR), a favored method of teaching a new language. My students had a wonderful time laughing at my antics, and most of them learned enough to make their way into intermediate ESL.

In an effort to keep the fun in the classroom, even during testing situations, I frequently broke the monotony of word tests by giving art tests. The students had to draw whatever I dictated. Of course, the dictation reflected the concepts and vocabulary in the lesson I had taught. The wilder my imagination, the more fun we had and the funnier the drawings turned out.

When I taught clothing and parts of the body, I had my students draw a boy and a girl. For the boy, I started from the head down. He had a big head, short hair, big, round black eyes, no eyebrows, small ears, a long body, very short legs, and big feet. For the girl, I started in reverse order: from her feet up. The girl had very small feet and wore high heels. She had long, thin legs, an A-line short skirt, a loose sweater with Mickey Mouse on it, long arms, a very long neck, a big head with a pointed chin. She could have round eyes or square eyes, possibly one of each. I could have added jewelry, a watch, which wrist the watch was on, and continued embellishing the picture until I ran out of vocabulary words. This technique can be applied to anything being taught: verbs, prepositions, adjectives. I sometimes brought in crayons so we could have colors in the drawings. If the students drew what I dictated, no matter how the picture looked, their grades were A's.

When I displayed the pictures on the walls, I found that the students were delighted to see their work on exhibition. Also, I began noticing an unexpected benefit: the students in my regular English class developed a fascination for the ESL drawings. They began asking me questions such as "What else do you teach? What is the meaning of these drawings? Are the students supposed to be drawing you?"

After explaining that my ESL students were struggling to learn simple words like "big" and "small," I noticed a subtle change in my native speakers. Many of those who had shown disdain and prejudice toward the immigrants began to take an interest in their progress and what they were learning, through watching the changing pictures. They became much more sympathetic toward the youngsters who were trying so hard to learn.

I am still teaching an ESL class, still without materials from the school district, but now I do not really need them—I have created my own program. I love hearing students who did not understand one word of English say, "Thank you," when I say, "I like your outfit." I feel proud when the youngster who was having so much trouble pronouncing everything comes up to me and says, with perfect enunciation, "May I please be excused to go to the bathroom?"

Editor

Kent Gill has led a long and productive career in education and public service. For thirty years, he taught English and history at Holmes Junior High School in Davis, California, from which he is now retired. At present he is a volunteer, teaching writing, at Black Butte School, Camp Sherman, Oregon. He took his B.A. from the University of Colorado in 1950; his M.Ed. from the University of Oregon in 1954; and a Certificate of Advanced Study from Harvard University in 1969. Among the many positions he has held in education are teacher-consultant, Area III English Project, California, 1963–68; teacher-consultant, Bay Area Writing Project, 1976; various roles with the Area III Writing Project, California; a member of the Writing Development Team, California Assessment Project, 1985–88. He is co-author (with Jackie Proett) of *The Writing Process in Action* (NCTE, 1986) and editor of the *Area III Third Report* (1966). He served as chair of the NCTE Committee on Classroom Practices, 1987–92. He has also served as president of the Sierra Club, 1974–76, and mayor of Davis, California, 1966–68.

Contributors

Kathy Allen is a reading and English-as-a-second-language teacher at Palos Verdes Intermediate School, Palos Verdes Estates, California. She has taught grades K–8, and she has been a reading and ESL methods teacher at the Graduate School of Education, University of California at Los Angeles. She is a fellow of the California Literature Project and the California Writing Project, and has led a summer institute on literature. She makes presentations regularly at CRA conventions, affiliate conferences, and various districts in Southern California. Her article "History in the Making: Writing for Real Audiences" was published in *English Journal*.

Dael Angelico-Hart has taught in the elementary classroom for eleven years and has been an elementary language arts specialist for two. As a teacher and coordinator of gifted and talented students, she has worked with students and teachers at levels K–8. She is the Discover Teacher at the Dunn Middle School in Danvers, Massachusetts, and presents whole language workshops at regional conferences, cities, and towns all across Massachusetts. She is currently working on a doctorate in language and literacy at the University of Massachusetts at Lowell.

Ronald Barron is an English teacher at Richfield High School in Richfield, Minnesota. He is a past president of the Minnesota Council of Teachers of English and is currently a member of the board of directors of the Minnesota Humanities Commission. He also served on the advisory board for the publication of *Braided Lives*, a multicultural literature anthology published jointly by the Minnesota Humanities Commission and the Minnesota Council of Teachers of English. In addition to articles in *ALAN Review, English Journal,* and *Minnesota English Journal,* he wrote *A Guide to Minnesota Authors* (1988), a book he is currently revising for an expanded second edition.

Susan Reese Brown teaches honors and regular freshman English at Durango High School, Durango, Colorado. She has taught Chapter 1 classes for seventh, eighth, and ninth graders as well as seventh-grade English. Her published articles include "How Will My Garden Grow?" and "How to Thaw an Iceberg," both on teaching.

Barbara Jones Brough has been teaching English at Anderson High School, Cincinnati, Ohio, for eighteen years, where she was named "Teacher of the Year" in 1991. She currently teaches advanced placement and college preparatory, senior-level English. She has coached the English 12 Scholastic Team for six years, winning the state championship four times. She has made presentations at the national conventions of the Council of English Leaders and the National Council of Teachers of English, as well as local scholastic banquets and board meetings. She was one of sixty educators from across the country to be selected to participate in Harvard University's "Institute on Reading, Writing, and Civic Education." A member of Cum Laude and MENSA, she has had articles published in *The Civic Perspective* and *Notes Plus*. Within her community, she is president of the Delta Psi Chapter of Delta Kappa Gamma, the professional women educators' honors society.

Jim Burke teaches English at Burlingame High School, Burlingame, California. He has taught English for three years and prior to that, taught in Tunisia with the Peace Corps. He has published many essays on educational issues; his poetry has appeared in various journals across the country. He has just finished his second novel, *On My Family's Case*, for which he is currently seeking an agent. He also serves as legislative chair for both the California Association of Teachers of English and the Central California Council of Teachers of English, and he writes a bimonthly column on educational legislation for *California English*.

Kathy Coffey has taught English at the University of Colorado, Metropolitan State College, and Regis University. She is currently working as a writer and editor. Her articles and poetry have appeared in *English Journal*, *Media and Methods*, and *Kentucky English Journal*. She has made presentations at NCTE and CLAS conventions. She recently nominated Janet Zanger, the subject of her essay in this volume, as Colorado Language Arts Teacher of the Year, and was pleased to attend her award reception with her two children, both former students of Mrs. Zanger's.

Thomas Dukes is associate professor of English at the University of Akron. He teaches business and professional writing, American and British literature, and freshman composition. In addition to writing on business communication pedagogy, he has published on Elizabeth Bowen, Rumer Godden, Penelope Lively, and Marjorie Kinnan Rawlings. He is currently editing a collection of essays on AIDS texts with Sheryl Stevenson.

Elise Ann Earthman is assistant professor of English at San Francisco State University, where she teaches in the secondary credential and M.A. in composition programs. Her area of special interest is the teaching of literature, and she has published her research in the areas of readers' responses to literature and reading and writing about literature in the college classroom. A finalist in the 1991 competition for NCTE's Promising Researcher Award, she regularly presents her work at the NCTE and CCCC annual conventions.

Theodore F. Fabiano is a language arts teacher at Blue Valley North High School, Overland Park, Kansas. He teaches freshman English, American literature, and British literature. He has presented at the Seattle and Louisville NCTE conventions, the CCCC convention in San Diego, and the writing conference in Kansas City.

Diann Gerke has been a teacher of secondary English for twenty-two years. She has taught in both rural and inner-city schools in Ohio and Michigan. She has been an active member of the Toledo Area Writing Project and is the high school editor for its newsletter. Her literary magazine *The Writings on the Wall* became an instrumental part of the U.S.S.R. and U.S. student exchange program in Toledo, with copies being sent to the State Department of Education, Volgograd, U.S.S.R.

F. Todd Goodson is completing his Ph.D. in English education at the University of Kansas. Previously, he taught English at Blue Valley North High School, Overland Park, Kansas. His work has appeared in *English Journal, Kansas English,* and *Oklahoma English Journal.*

Sarah K. Herz has taught English in grades 7–12 in Westport, Connecticut, for twenty years. Her recent sabbatical focused on using young adult literature with required classics. Herz presents workshops in YAL at regional and state reading and English conferences, as well as staff development workshops in various school districts. She is a recipient of fellowships from the National Endowment for the Humanities, the Yale Teachers' Institute, and the Connecticut Writing Project. She is on the boards of the Connecticut Council of Teachers of English and the New England Association of Teachers of English. She is working on a book about YAL and the classics.

Larry R. Johannessen is assistant professor of English and director of English education at Saint Xavier University, Chicago, Illinois. He taught high school English for twelve years and has directed workshops and inservice programs for teachers in writing, thinking, and literature instruction. He was a participant, representing secondary teachers, in the English Coalition Conference in 1987. In addition to his journal articles, book chapters, and textbooks, he is author of *Illumination Rounds: Teaching the Literature of the Vietnam War* (NCTE, 1992) and co-author (with Elizabeth A. Kahn and Carolyn Calhoun Walter) of two popular NCTE publications: *Writing about Literature* (1984) and *Designing and Sequencing Prewriting Activities* (1982). He is a frequent speaker at NCTE conventions and affiliate conferences.

Joel Kammer has taught high school English for fourteen years in Santa Rosa, California. He has served as English department chair at two schools, and has worked as a school restructuring research specialist as well as a district mentor teacher. He was involved in the development of California's CAP writing assessment program and, in 1987, was chosen to spend five weeks in Stratford, England, as an NEH fellow. He has been a presenter at CATE conferences and has published articles on school restructuring and teaching literature in *California English.* Currently, he is teaching humanities and sciences courses in a uniquely restructured learning community within Piner High School, Santa Rosa, California.

Gerald F. Luboff is a professor of English at the County College of Morris. In addition to teaching courses in writing and American literature, he has been a frequent seminar participant at conferences of the Hemingway Society, of which he is a member, and a presenter at the Conference on College Composition and Communication. He is currently working on a translation of a contemporary French novel.

Beverly A. McColley teaches English at Norfolk Academy, Norfolk, Virginia. She has taught English and Latin for twenty years, having spent thirteen years teaching in the Virginia Beach City Public Schools. In 1990, the Virginia Beach Association of Teachers of English voted her Teacher of the Year, and the Virginia Association of Teachers of English has twice recognized her for outstanding service to the English profession. She received a master's degree from the Bread Loaf School of English, Middlebury College, and spent three summers studying at Lincoln College, Oxford. She has published articles in *English Journal, Classroom Practices, New Jersey English Journal,* and the *Computer-Assisted Composition Journal.*

Carol Meinhardt is an English teacher at Springfield High School, Springfield, Pennsylvania, and co-director of the Lehigh Valley Writing Project at Pennsylvania State University at Allentown. A writer and former book editor, she shares her experience with her students in a total reading-writing workshop program in the high school classroom. At present, she is making a film of her students working in that environment.

G. Douglas Meyers is chair of the English department at the University of Texas at El Paso, where he previously directed the freshman composition program. He has taught at the University of Maryland and Florida International University and has worked as a K–12 language arts consultant in Central America. A former high school English teacher, he has also directed a National Writing Project site, has published widely, and has made numerous conference presentations on topics related to the teaching of writing and English education.

JoAnna Stephens Mink is assistant professor of English at Mankato State University. She is co-editor of *Joinings and Disjoinings: The Significance of Marital Status in Literature* (1991) and *The Significance of Sibling Relationships in Literature* (forthcoming). She has presented papers at conferences of the Midwest Modern Language Association, the Conference on College Composition and Communication, and others. Her articles have appeared in *Heroines of Popular Culture, Literature and Life: Making Connections in the Classroom* (NCTE, 1990), *Teaching English in the Two-Year College, North Carolina English Teacher,* and *Illinois English Bulletin,* among others. At present, she is working on two anthologies, one on the relationship between communication and women's friendship in literature, and another on feminist collaboration. Her current research interests include family relationships and the changing role of women in the nineteenth century.

William R. Mollineaux is a seventh-grade English teacher and coordinator of English at Sedgwick Middle School, West Hartford, Connecticut. As a member of the board of directors of the Connecticut Council of Teachers of English, he is membership chair, liaison officer to NCTE, and past chair of the 1991 Spring Conference. He has presented workshops on writing, mainstreaming special education students, using young adult literature in the classroom, and being an effective team leader at conferences sponsored by the New England League of Middle Schools, the New England Association of Teachers of English, and area TAWL groups. In 1990, he and his wife were the first husband-wife team to become celebrants in the State of Connecticut's Celebration of Excellence program.

Perry Oldham is English chair at Casady School, a preparatory school in Oklahoma City. In addition to making regular presentations at professional conferences, he has published poetry in periodicals and anthologies including *New Directions* and *Webster Review,* and he has published a novel, *Higher Ground* (1987).

Rose Cherie Reissman is a curriculum specialist and multicultural specialist in Community School District 25, Flushing, New York. She is a member of the Impact II Teacher to Teacher Network, an adjunct professor of education at Manhattanville College, and president-elect of NYCATE. Her articles have appeared in *English Journal, Educational Leadership, Teacher's Journal, The Reading Teacher,* and *The Computing Teacher.* She makes presentations regularly at NCTE conventions, LRE education sites, and Impact II conferences.

Rose Rosenthal teaches English, English as a second language, and journalism at Morningside High School, Inglewood, California. She is a fellow of the California Writing Project and has edited many writing magazines. She designed and served as director of a "Space Age" school-within-a-school program which unified the high school curriculum around future studies.

Joanna Schultz teaches English at the Ellis School, Pittsburgh, Pennsylvania. During summers, she has taught creative writing to adolescents in summer schools, Western Pennsylvania Writing Project programs, and most recently, at the Carnegie Museum of Art. During after-school hours, she has worked as an inservice consultant, specializing in using writing to teach literature, at area middle and high schools. She has presented workshops on the reading-writing connection, on gender studies, and on poetry writing in the classroom at local, state, and mid-Atlantic states conferences. She is on the executive board of the Western Pennsylvania Writing Project and has recently completed a master's thesis at the University of Pittsburgh, a two-year study on how eighth graders use classroom journals to make meaning of the literature they read, of themselves, and of the world around them.

Edythe H. Schwartz is a lecturer in child development in the School of Education, California State University at Sacramento, where she teaches courses in the undergraduate child development major and supervises student teachers in the multiple subjects credential program. She has authored a fifteen-article newspaper series on parenting, has presented workshops at national and state conferences of the Association for the Education of Young Children, is a member of the CSUS Writing in the Disciplines program, and serves as a teacher-consultant for the Area III Writing Project.

Phyllis B. Schwartz is the English department head at Lord Byng Secondary School, Vancouver, British Columbia, Canada. She is a member of the English and Language Arts Curriculum Revision Working Committee for the Ministry of Education, British Columbia. She is one of the four authors of *Learning through Reading,* a teachers' resource for teaching reading across the curriculum. Recently, two of her articles on using film in the English classroom have been republished in *Animando to Zea,* a compendium of teaching ideas for film educators published by the National Film Board of Canada. For the past two years, she has been a site development coordinator for Ministry of Education projects related to Year 2000 Curriculum and Programme Development.

Daniel D. Victor is a teacher of English at Fairfax High School, Los Angeles, California. In addition to having taught for twenty-six years, he has served as a mentor teacher, a supervising teacher, and a workshop leader for such organizations as the Los Angeles Unified School District, the College Board, and NCTE. Holder of a Ph.D. in American literature from the Claremont Graduate School, he is a two-time participant in NEH-sponsored summer seminars, one at Berkeley, California, another at Oxford University, England; a winner of the Council for Basic Education's Independent Study Grant, and co-editor of its magazine *Scholarly Adventures.* His first novel, *The Seventh Bullet,* was published in 1992.

Gary A. Watson is an English and writing teacher at Butler Traditional/ Technical High School, Louisville, Kentucky. He has taught high school English for fifteen years. Currently, he is teaching theatre arts and serving as writing resource teacher for the Reason for Writing Project at Butler. In addition to the present volume, he has published in the *Quarterly* of the National Writing Project. He also facilitates writing inservices and makes presentations before local and state conferences.

Beverly Wilkins has been teaching English and history for twenty years. In 1992 she received her M.S. Ed. in curriculum and instruction with an endorsement in gifted and talented education from Baylor University. In addition to her teaching assignment at Midway Middle School, Waco, Texas, she is a freelance writer, specializing in historical topics. She is also a National Writing Project fellow and conducts writing workshops for local school districts. She has made several presentations at the Texas Association for the Improvement of Reading (TAIR) and Baylor University's National Writing Project.

Myra Zarnowski is an associate professor in the Department of Elementary and Early Childhood Education at Queens College, CUNY. She is the author of *Learning about Biographies: A Reading-and-Writing Approach for Children* (NCTE, 1990) and co-editor of the forthcoming *Children's Literature and Social Studies: Selecting and Using Notable Books in the Classroom*. At present, she is serving as a member of the NCTE Committee on Communicating Research-Based Knowledge of Language Learning and Curriculum to School Administrators.

Titles in the Classroom Practices in Teaching English Series

NCTE began publishing the Classroom Practices series in 1963 with *Promising Practices in the Teaching of English*. Volumes 1–16 and Volumes 18–20 of the series are out of print. The following titles are available through the NCTE *Catalog*.